Book and CD for B♭, E♭, C and Bass Clef Instruments

Arranged and Produced by Mark Taylor

BOOK

CD

ISBN 978-1-4584-2219-4

7777 W. Bluemound Rd. P.O. Box 13819 Milwaukee, WI 53213

Visit Hal Leonard Online at
www.halleonard.com

JOHN COLTRANE STANDARDS

Volume 163

Arranged and Produced
by Mark Taylor

Featured Players:

Graham Breedlove–Trumpet
John Desalme–Sax
Tony Nalker–Piano
Jim Roberts–Guitar
Paul Henry–Bass
Todd Harrison–Drums

Recorded at Bias Studios, Springfield, Virginia
Bob Dawson, Engineer

HOW TO USE THE CD:

Each song has two tracks:

1) Split Track/Melody

Woodwind, Brass, Keyboard, and **Mallet Players** can use this track as a learning tool for melody style and inflection.

Bass Players can learn and perform with this track – remove the recorded bass track by turning down the volume on the LEFT channel.

Keyboard and **Guitar Players** can learn and perform with this track – remove the recorded piano part by turning down the volume on the RIGHT channel.

2) Full Stereo Track

Soloists or **Groups** can learn and perform with this accompaniment track with the RHYTHM SECTION only.

CD

ALL OR NOTHING AT ALL

WORDS BY JACK LAWRENCE
MUSIC BY ARTHUR ALTMAN

C VERSION

MEDIUM LATIN

PIANO

PLAY

mf

SWING
Dmi7/C
G7(b5)/C
Cma7
Bbmi7
Eb7
Abma7
Bbmi7
Eb7
Bbmi7
Eb7
Bbmi7
C7(b9)
Fmi7
/Eb
Db7
C7
Bb7(b5)
LATIN
Ami(ma7)
Ami6
Ami(ma7)
Ami6
Ami(ma7)
Ami6
Bb7
Gmi7
Dmi7
E7(#9)
SWING
Ami(ma7)
Bb7
C6
Bbmi7
Eb7
Abma7

Bbmi7 Eb7

Bbmi7 Eb7 Bbmi7 Db7 C7(b5)

Fmi7 /Eb Db7 C7 Bb7(b5)

LATIN

Ami(MA7) Ami6 Ami(MA7) Ami6

Ami(MA7) Ami6 Bb7

Gmi7 Dmi7 E7(#9)

Ami(MA7) Bb7 C6 Bb7

C6 Bb7 C6 Bb7

C6 Bb7 C6 Bb7

C6 Bb7 C6 Bb7 CMA7(b5)

CD

11 : SPLIT TRACK/MELODY

12 : FULL STEREO TRACK

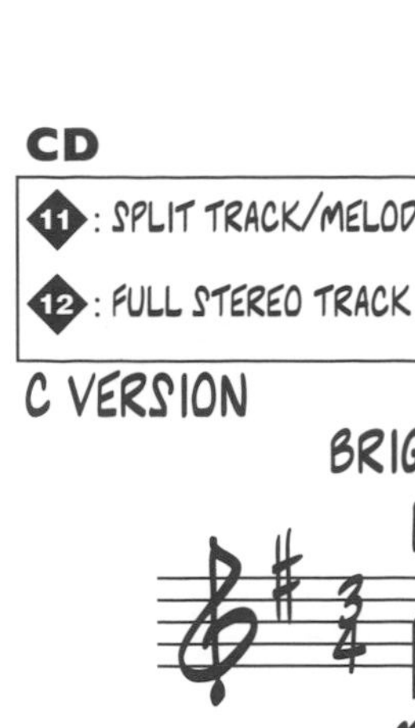

MY FAVORITE THINGS

LYRICS BY OSCAR HAMMERSTEIN II
MUSIC BY RICHARD RODGERS

C VERSION

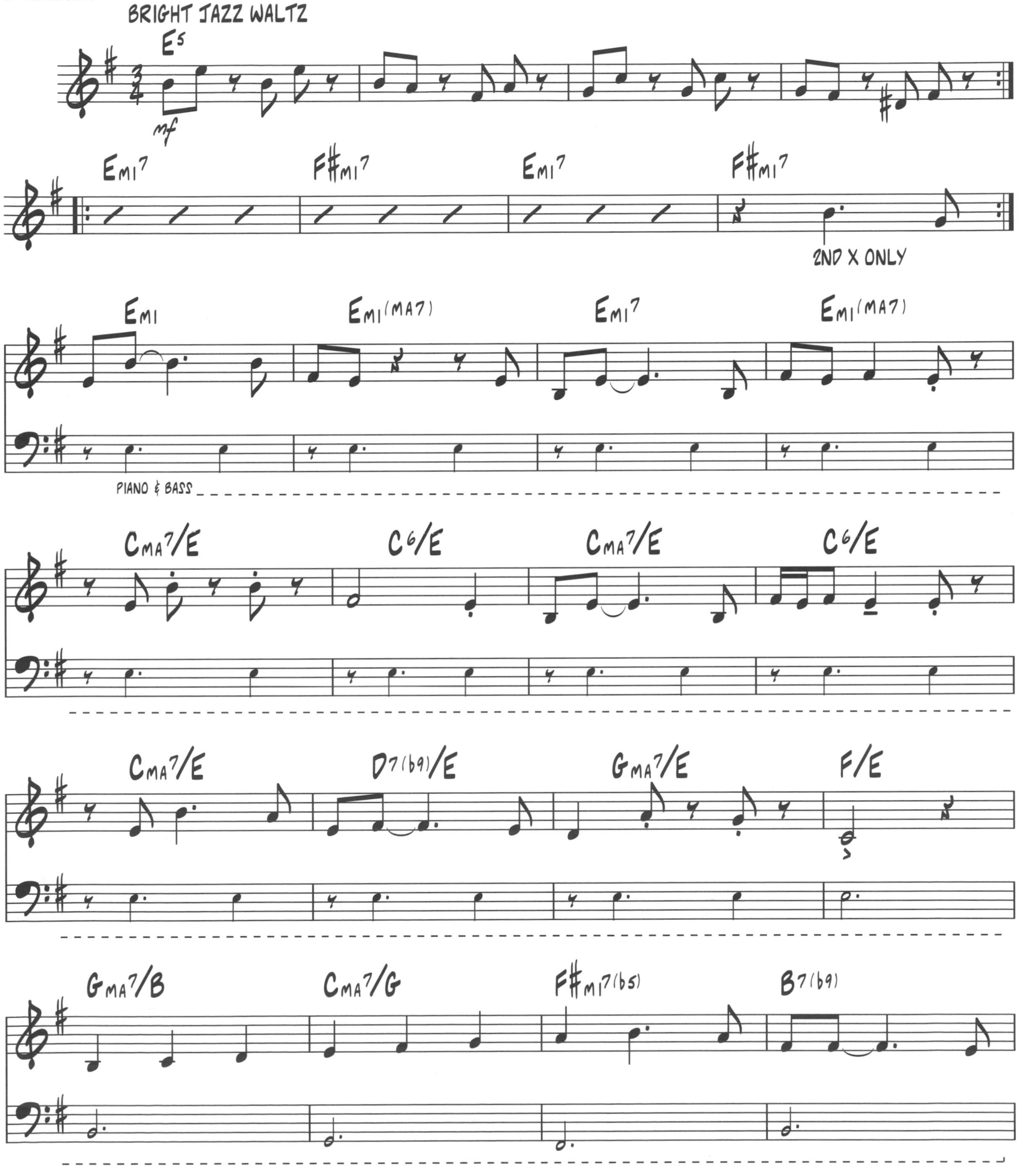

BRIGHT JAZZ WALTZ
E5
mf
Emi7
F#mi7
Emi7
F#mi7
2ND X ONLY
Emi
Emi(ma7)
Emi7
Emi(ma7)
PIANO & BASS
Cma7/E
C6/E
Cma7/E
C6/E
Cma7/E
D7(b9)/E
Gma7/E
F/E
Gma7/B
Cma7/G
F#mi7(b5)
B7(b9)

EMI7 F♯MI7 EMI7 F♯MI7
EMI7 F♯MI7 EMI7 F♯MI7
SOLO (PLAY 12X'S)
EMI7 F♯MI7 EMI7 F♯MI7
LAST X ONLY
EMI EMI(MA7) EMI7 EMI(MA7)
CMA7/E C6/E CMA7/E C6/E
3
CMA7/E D7(b9)/E GMA7/E F/E
GMA7/B CMA7/G F♯MI7(b5) B7(b9)
EMA7 F♯MI7 EMA7 F♯MI7
EMA7 F♯MI7 EMA7 F♯MI7
SOLO (PLAY 12X'S)
EMA7 F♯MI7 EMA7 F♯MI7
LAST X ONLY

EMA7
F#MI7/E
EMA7
F#MI7/E
3
AMA7/E
BMI7/E
AMA7/E
BMI7/E
3
CMA7/E
D7(b9)/E
GMA7/E
F/E
GMA7/B
CMA7/G
F#MI7(b5)
B7(b9)
EMI7
F#MI7(b5)
B7(b9)
EMI7
CMA7
BMI7
CMA7
BMI7
EMI7
A7
EMI7
AMI7
D7(b9)
6
BMI7
CMA7
BMI7
CMA7
1ST X ONLY
SOLO
EMI7
F#MI7
EMI7
F#MI7
EMI7

CD

3 : SPLIT TRACK/MELODY

4 : FULL STEREO TRACK

C VERSION

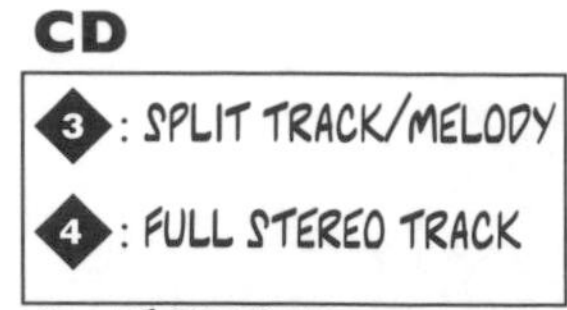

BUT NOT FOR ME

MUSIC AND LYRICS BY GEORGE GERSHWIN
AND IRA GERSHWIN

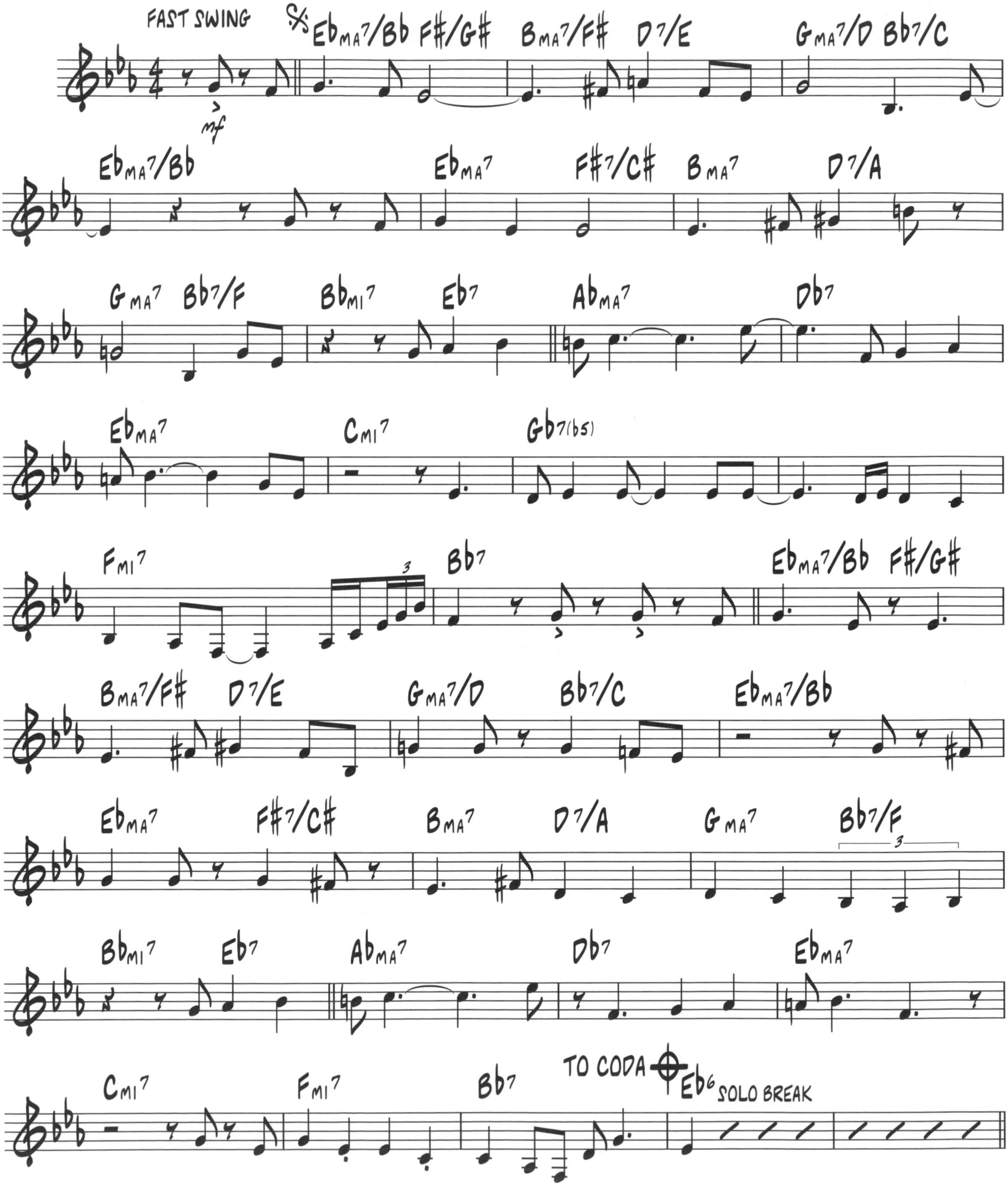
FAST SWING
mf
Ebma7/Bb F#/G# Bma7/F# D7/E Gma7/D Bb7/C
Ebma7/Bb Ebma7 F#7/C# Bma7 D7/A
Gma7 Bb7/F Bbmi7 Eb7 Abma7 Db7
Ebma7 Cmi7 Gb7(b5)
Fmi7 3 Bb7 Ebma7/Bb F#/G#
Bma7/F# D7/E Gma7/D Bb7/C Ebma7/Bb
Ebma7 F#7/C# Bma7 D7/A Gma7 Bb7/F 3
Bbmi7 Eb7 Abma7 Db7 Ebma7
Cmi7 Fmi7 Bb7 TO CODA Eb6 SOLO BREAK

SOLOS (2 CHORUSES)
Ebma7/Bb F#/G# Bma7/F# D7/E Gma7/D Bb7/C Ebma7/Bb
Ebma7 F#7/C# Bma7 D7/A Gma7 Bb7/F Bbmi7 Eb7
Abma7 Db7 Ebma7 Cmi7
Gb7(b5) Fmi7 Bb7
Ebma7/Bb F#/G# Bma7/F# D7/E Gma7/D Bb7/C Ebma7/Bb
Ebma7 F#7/C# Bma7 D7/A Gma7 Bb7/F Bbmi7 Eb7
Abma7 Db7 Ebma7 Cmi7
Fmi7 Bb7 Eb6 D.S. AL CODA
LAST X ONLY
CODA
N.C. Abmi7 Db7 Gmi7 C+7(#9)
PIANO
Fmi7 Bb7sus Bb7(b9) Ebma7

CD

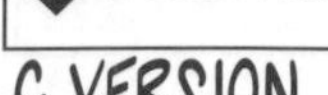

C VERSION

GREENSLEEVES

TRADITIONAL
ARRANGED BY McCOY TYNER

BbMA7
A7
DMI7
CMA7
BbMA7
A7
SOLO (4X'S)
DMI7
Eb7(b5)
1ST X ONLY
DMI7
CMA7
BbMA7
A7
DMI7
CMA7
BbMA7
A7
SOLO (4X'S)
DMI7
Eb7(b5)
DMI7
Eb7(b5)
DMI7
PIANO
1ST X ONLY
BASS

CD

7: SPLIT TRACK/MELODY

8: FULL STEREO TRACK

C VERSION

IN A SENTIMENTAL MOOD

BY DUKE ELLINGTON

MEDIUM BALLAD

Bbmi7

PIANO & BASS

PLAY

mf

Bbmi7

Ebmi7 Cmi7(b5) F7(b9) Bbmi7

Bb7 Ebmi7 Ab7(b9) Db6 Bbmi7

Ebmi7 Cmi7(b5) F7(b9)

Bbmi7 Bb7 Ebmi7 Ab7(b9)

Db6 Bmi7 E7 Ama7 F#mi7 Bmi7 E7 /D

A6/C# C7(b9) Bmi7 E7 Ama7 F#mi7
Bmi7 E7 Ab7sus Ab7(b9)
Bbmi7 Ebmi7
Cmi7(b5) F7(b9) Bbmi7 Bb7 TO CODA
Ebmi7 Ab7(b9) Db6 Cmi7(b5) F7(b9)
SOLO
Bbmi Bbmi(ma7) Bbmi7 Bbmi6 Ebmi Ebmi(ma7)
Ebmi7 Cmi7(b5) F7(b9) Bbmi /Ab Gmi7(b5) Gbma7 Fmi7 Bb7
1. 2. D.S. AL CODA
Ebmi7 Ab7(b9) Db6 Cmi7(b5) F7(b9) Db6 Bmi7 E7
CODA Ebmi7 Ab7(b9) Db6
PIANO

CD

LUSH LIFE

WORDS AND MUSIC BY
BILLY STRAYHORN

C VERSION

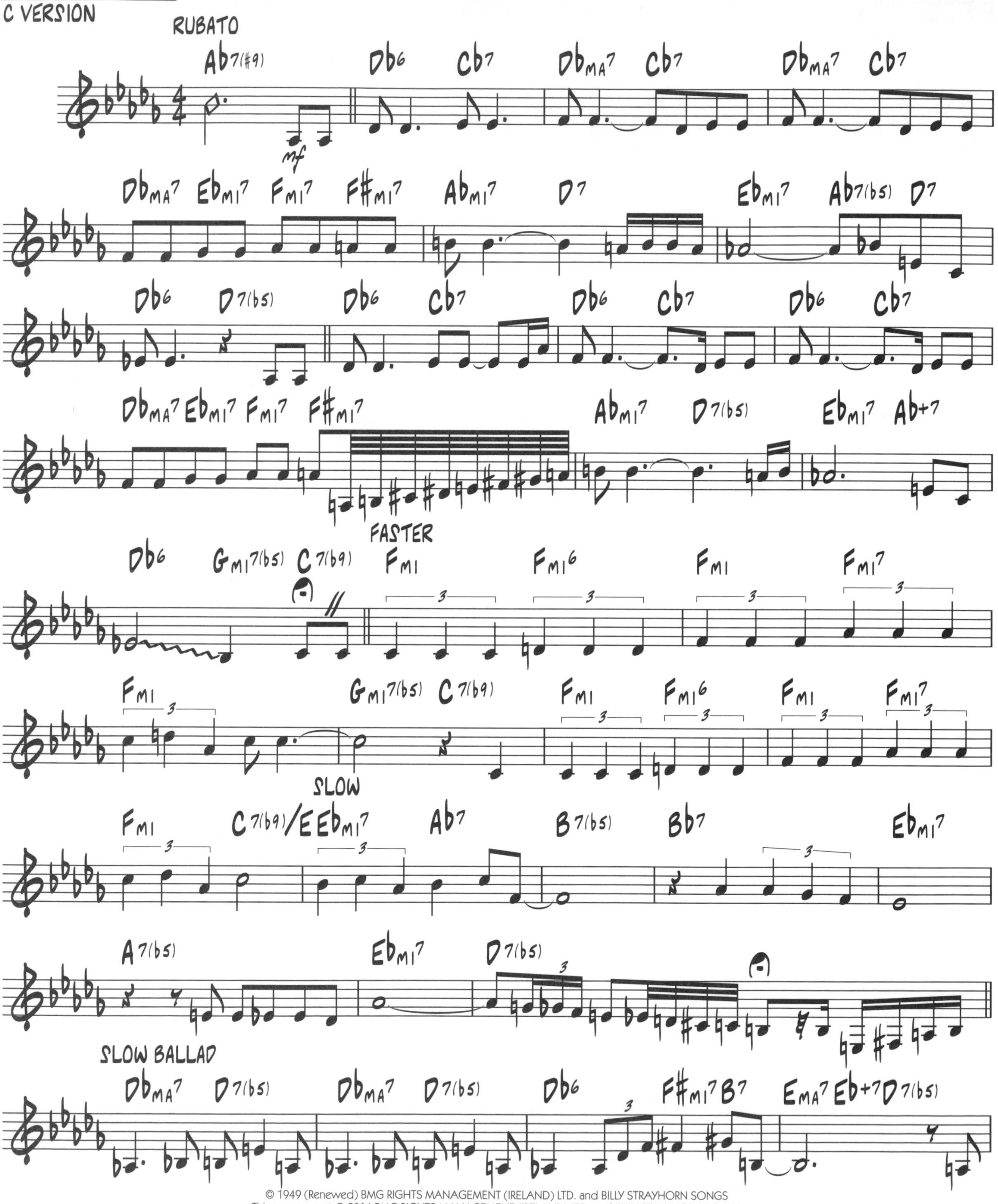

RUBATO

FASTER

SLOW

SLOW BALLAD

DbMA7 D7(b5) DbMA7 D7(b5) Db6 Db7 C7 FMA7 A+7
AbMA7 Eb+7(#9) AbMA7 EMI7 A7 DMA7 DMI7 G7 CMA7 Ab7
DbMA7 D7(b5) DbMA7 D7(b5) Db6 C7(#9)(b5) B7
Bb7SUS Bb7(b9) F#MI7 B7 A+7 Ab7 DbMA7 Gb7
TO CODA
FMI7 Bb7 F#MI7 B7 A+7 Ab7
DBL. TIME FEEL
SOLO
Ab7(#9) A7(#9) Bb7(#9) B7(#9) C7(#9) D7(b5) DbMA7 Ab7 DbMA7 D7(b5) DbMA7 D7(b5)
DbMA7 D7(b5) DbMA7 D7(b5) Db6 F#MI7 B7 EMA7 Eb+7 D7(b5)
DbMA7 D7(b5) DbMA7 D7(b5) Db6 Db7 C7 FMA7
D.S. AL CODA
AbMA7 Eb+7(#9) AbMA7 EMI7 A7 DMA7 DMI7 G7 CMA7 Ab7
CODA
Ab7(#9) A7(#9) Bb7(#9) B7(#9) C7(#9) D7(b5) DbMA7

MY ONE AND ONLY LOVE

WORDS BY ROBERT MELLIN
MUSIC BY GUY WOOD

C VERSION

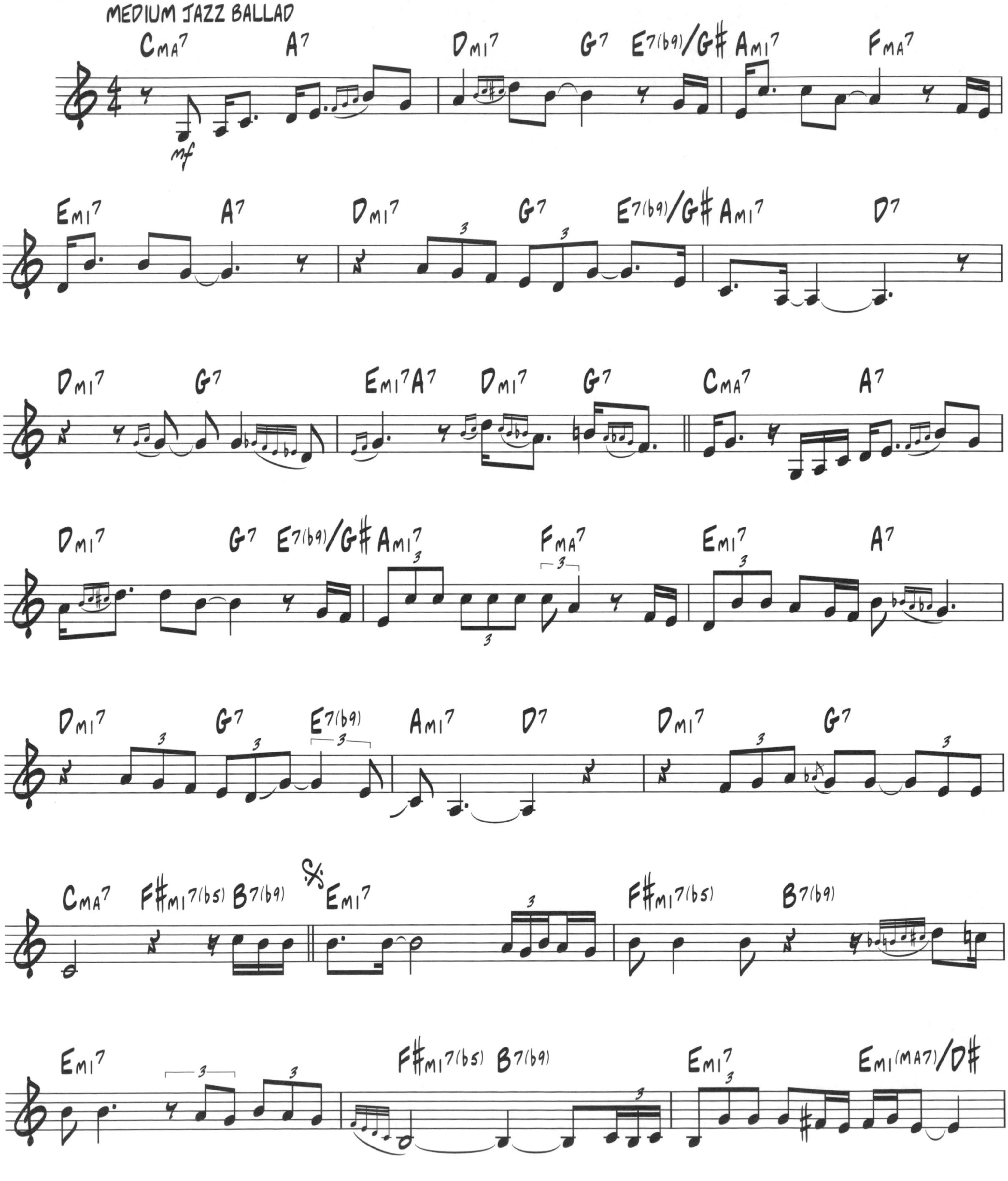

MEDIUM JAZZ BALLAD

EMI7/D C#MI7(b5) DMI7 G7(b9)
CMA7 A7 DMI7 G7 E7(b9)/G# AMI7 FMA7
EMI7 A7 DMI7 G7 E7(b9)/G# AMI7 D7(b9)
DMI7 G7 TO CODA CMA7/G G7
SOLO
CMA7 A7 DMI7 G7 E7(b9)/G# AMI7 FMA7
1ST X ONLY
EMI7 A7 DMI7 G7 E7(b9)/G# AMI7 D7
DMI7 G7
1. EMI7 A7 DMI7 G7
2. CMA7 F#MI7(b5) B7(b9)
D.S. AL CODA
CODA
CMA7/G G7 CMA7

CD

15: SPLIT TRACK/MELODY
16: FULL STEREO TRACK

C VERSION

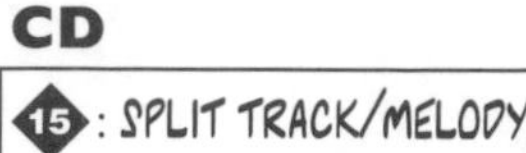

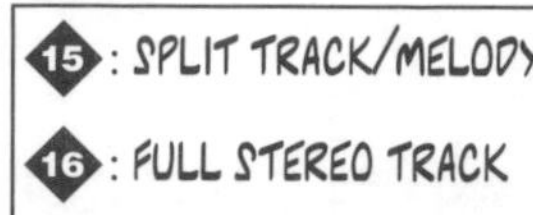

MY SHINING HOUR

LYRIC BY JOHNNY MERCER
MUSIC BY HAROLD ARLEN

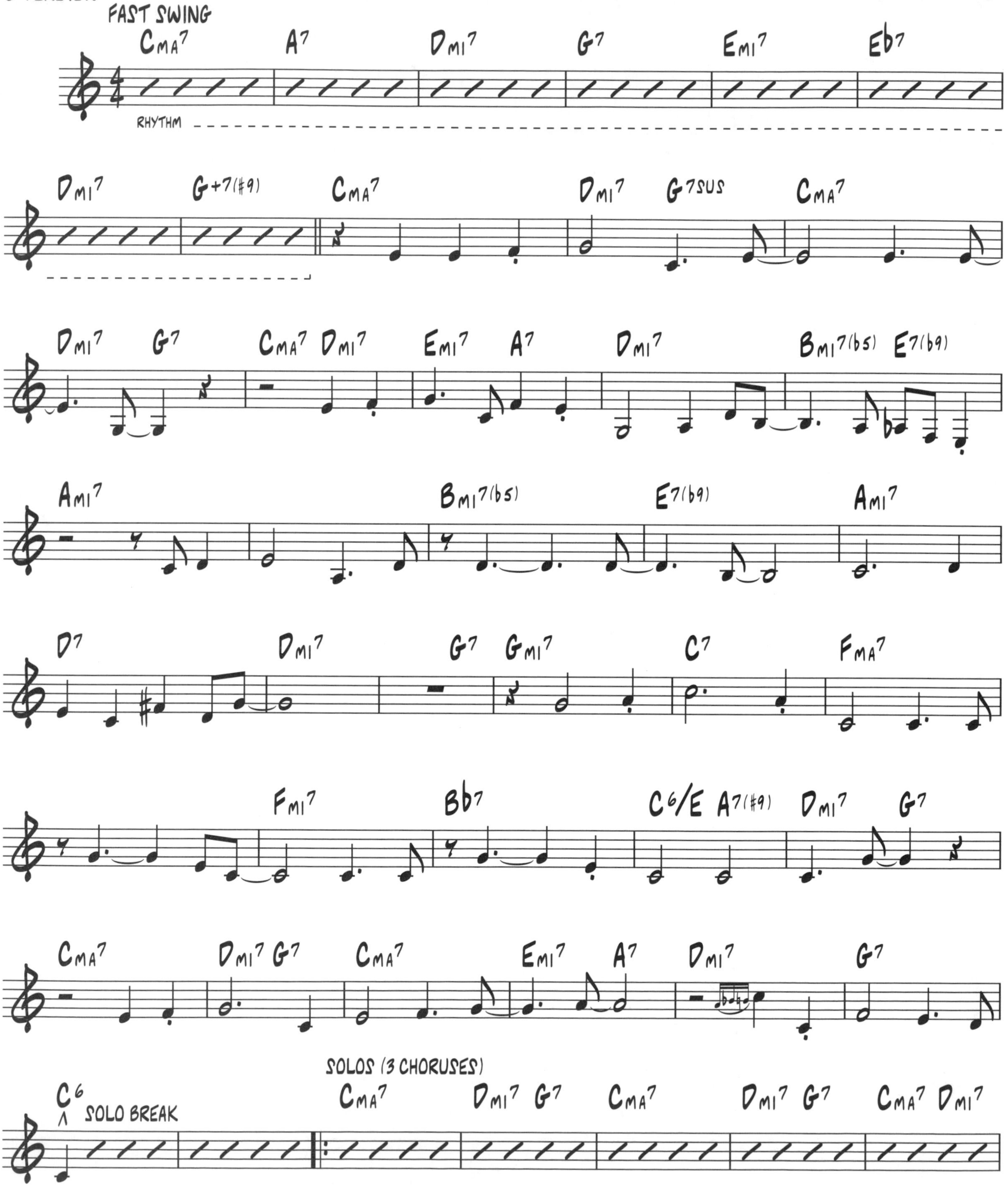

FAST SWING
CMA7 A7 DMI7 G7 EMI7 Eb7
RHYTHM
DMI7 G+7(#9) CMA7 DMI7 G7SUS CMA7
DMI7 G7 CMA7 DMI7 EMI7 A7 DMI7 BMI7(b5) E7(b9)
AMI7 BMI7(b5) E7(b9) AMI7
D7 DMI7 G7 GMI7 C7 FMA7
FMI7 Bb7 C6/E A7(#9) DMI7 G7
CMA7 DMI7 G7 CMA7 EMI7 A7 DMI7 G7
SOLOS (3 CHORUSES)
C6 SOLO BREAK
CMA7 DMI7 G7 CMA7 DMI7 G7 CMA7 DMI7

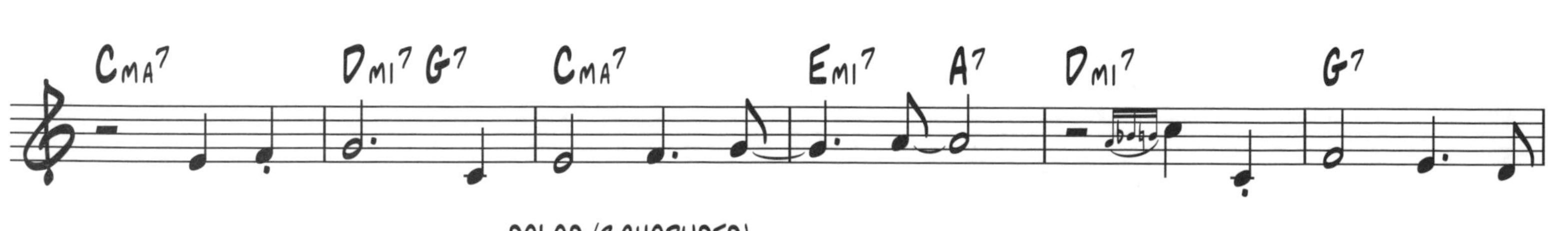

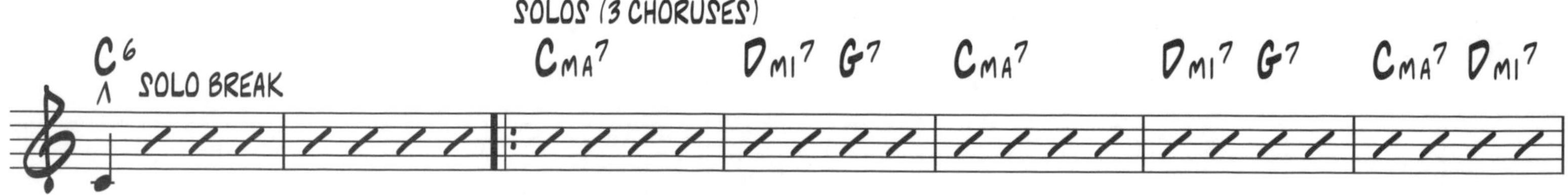

Emi7 A7 Dmi7 Bmi7(b5) E7(b9) Ami7 Bmi7(b5)
E7(b9) Ami7 D7(b5) Dmi7 G7 Gmi7 C7
Fma7 Fmi7 Bb7 C6/E A7 Dmi7 G7 Cma7
Dmi7 G7 Cma7 Emi7 A7 Dmi7 G7 C6 Dmi7 G7
Cma7 Dmi7 G7sus Cma7 Dmi7 G7 Cma7 Dmi7 Emi7 A7
Dmi7 Bmi7(b5) E7(b9) Ami7 Bmi7(b5) E7(b9)
Ami7 D7 Dmi7 G7 Gmi7 C7
Fma7 Fmi7 Bb7 C6/E A7 Dmi7 G7
Cma7 Dmi7 G7 Cma7 Emi7 A7 Dmi7 G7
Fmi7 Bb7 Emi7 A7 Dmi7 G7 C6 Cma7(b5)

THE NIGHT HAS A THOUSAND EYES

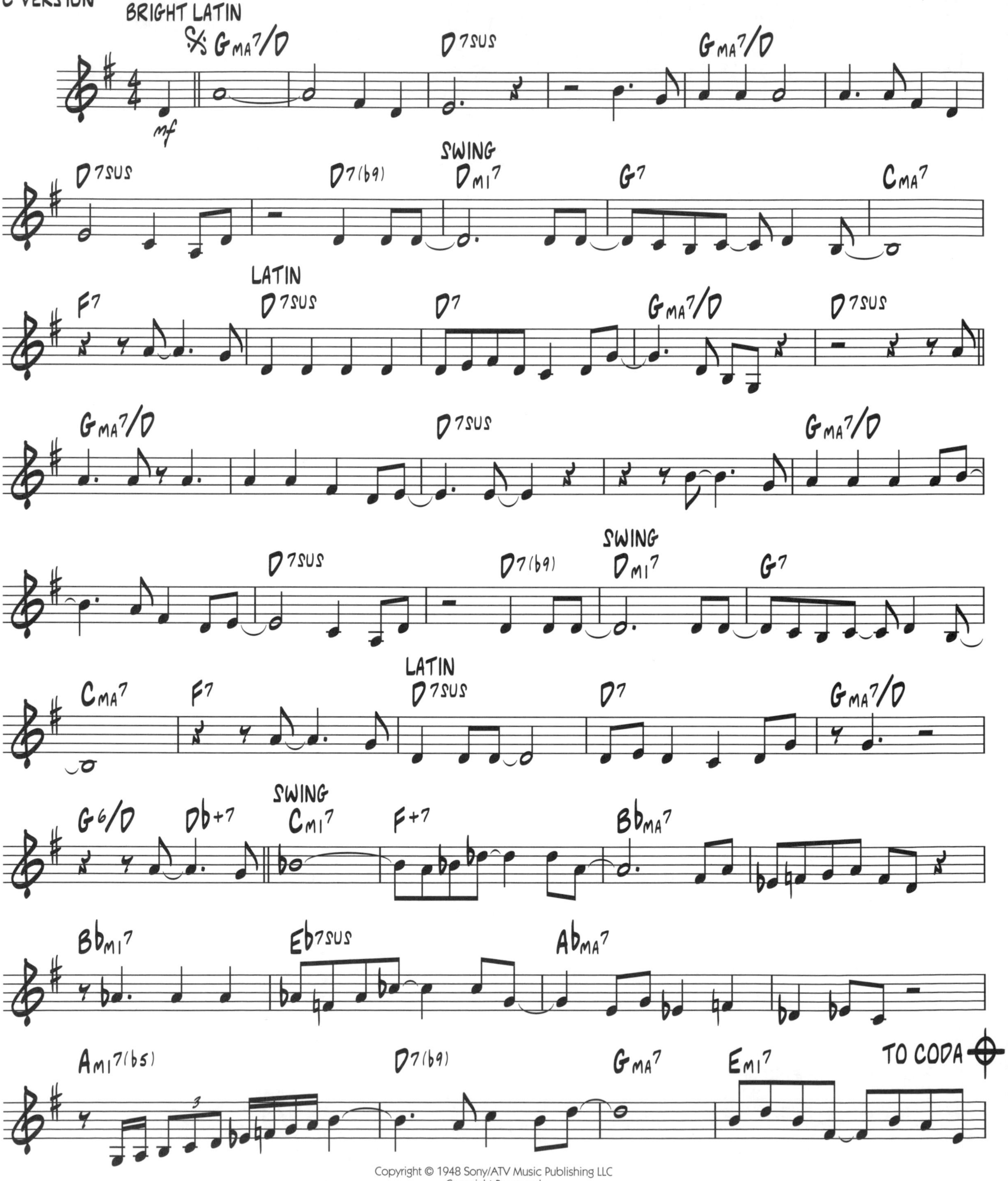

WORDS BY BUDDY BERNIER
MUSIC BY JERRY BRAININ

BRIGHT LATIN

LATIN
D7SUS
D7
GMA7/D
G6
D7SUS
D7
GMA7/D
G6/D
SOLO BREAK
LATIN
SOLO
GMA7/D
D7SUS
GMA7/D
D7SUS
D7(b9)
SWING
DMI7
G7
CMA7
F7
LATIN
D7SUS
D7
GMA7/D
1.
D7SUS
2.
G6/D Db7
SWING
CMI7
F+7
BbMA7
BbMI7
Eb7
AbMA7
AMI7(b5)
D7(b9)
GMA7
EMI7
LATIN
D7SUS
D7
GMA7/D
G6/D
D7SUS
D7
GMA7/D
D.S. AL CODA
G6/D
CODA
D7SUS
D7
GMA7/D
G6/D
D7SUS
D7
GMA7/D
G6/D
D7SUS
D7
AMI7/D
Bbo7/D
AMI7/D
Abo7/D
AMI7/D
D7(b9)
GMA7

CD

19: SPLIT TRACK/MELODY

20: FULL STEREO TRACK

C VERSION

SOFTLY AS IN A MORNING SUNRISE

LYRICS BY OSCAR HAMMERSTEIN II
MUSIC BY SIGMUND ROMBERG

SOLOS (3 CHORUSES)
CMI7 DMI7(b5) G+7 CMI7 DMI7(b5) G+7
CMI7 DMI7(b5) G+7 CMI7 Db7(b5) DMI7(b5) G+7(#9)
CMI7 DMI7(b5) G+7 CMI7 DMI7(b5) G+7
CMI7 DMI7(b5) G+7 CMI7 FMI7 Bb7
EbMA7 Db7(b5) C7(b9)
FMI7 F#07 D7(#9) G+7
CMI7 DMI7(b5) G+7 CMI7 DMI7(b5) G+7
D.C. AL CODA
CMI7 DMI7(b5) G+7 CMI7 Db7(b5) DMI7(b5) Db7(b5)
CODA
N.C.
CMI(MA7)
DRUMS

ALL OR NOTHING AT ALL

WORDS BY JACK LAWRENCE
MUSIC BY ARTHUR ALTMAN

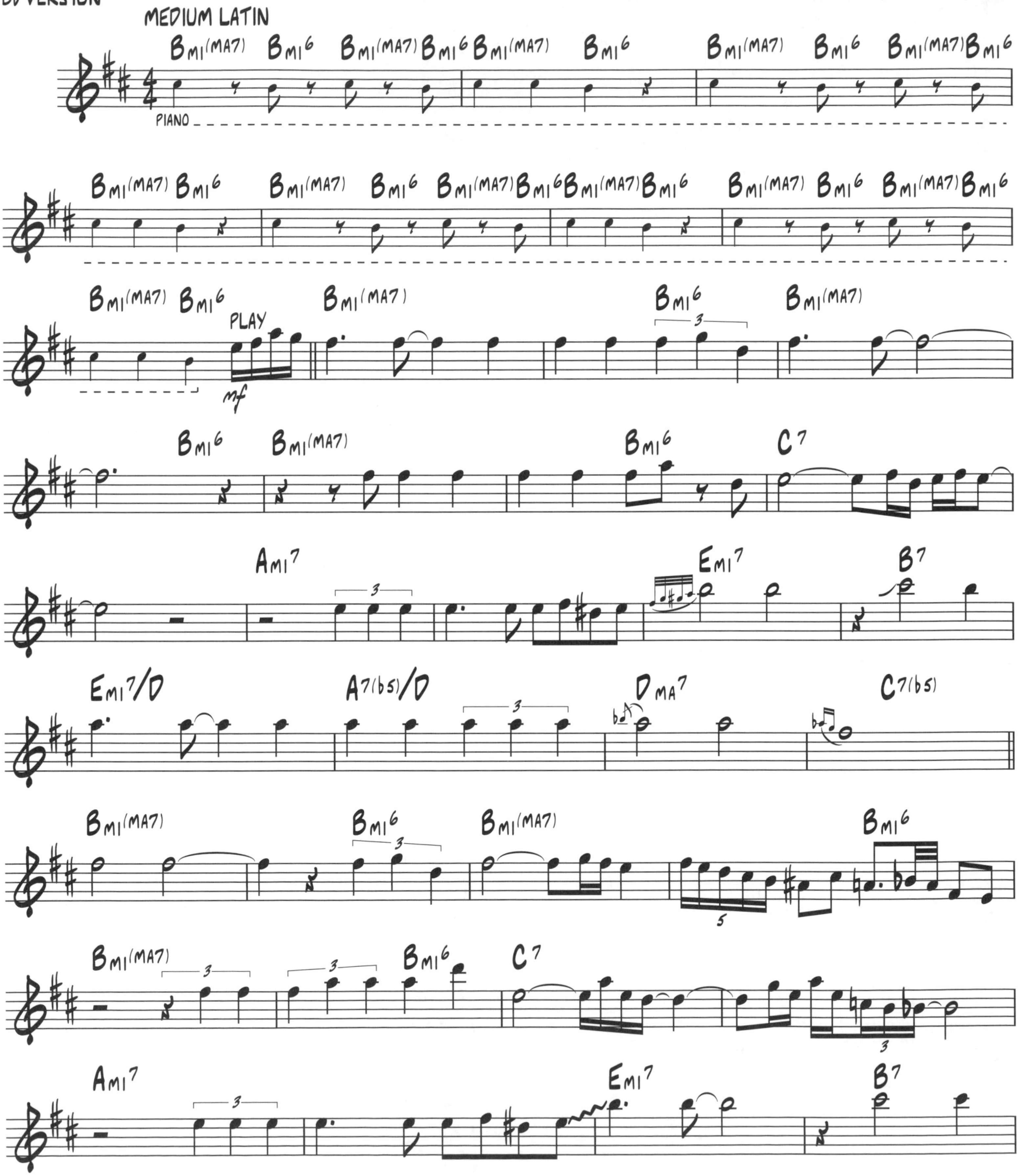

MEDIUM LATIN

EMI7/D
A7(b5)/D
DMA7
SWING
CMI7
F7
BbMA7
CMI7
F7
CMI7
F7
CMI7
D7(b9)
GMI7
/F
Eb7
D7
C7(b5)
LATIN
BMI(MA7)
BMI6
BMI(MA7)
BMI6
BMI(MA7)
BMI6
C7
AMI7
EMI7
F#7(#9)
BMI(MA7)
C7
D6
SWING
CMI7
F7
BbMA7

CMI7
F7
CMI7
F7
CMI7
Eb7
D7(b5)
GMI7
/F
Eb7
D7
C7(b5)
LATIN
BMI(MA7)
BMI6
BMI(MA7)
BMI6
BMI(MA7)
BMI6
C7
AMI7
EMI7
F#7(#9)
BMI(MA7)
C7
D6
C7
D6
C7
D6
C7
D6
C7
D6
C7
D6
C7
D6
C7
DMA7(b5)

CD

11 : SPLIT TRACK/MELODY

12 : FULL STEREO TRACK

Bb VERSION

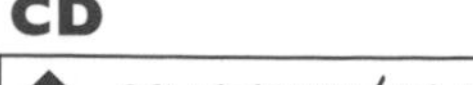

MY FAVORITE THINGS

LYRICS BY OSCAR HAMMERSTEIN II
MUSIC BY RICHARD RODGERS

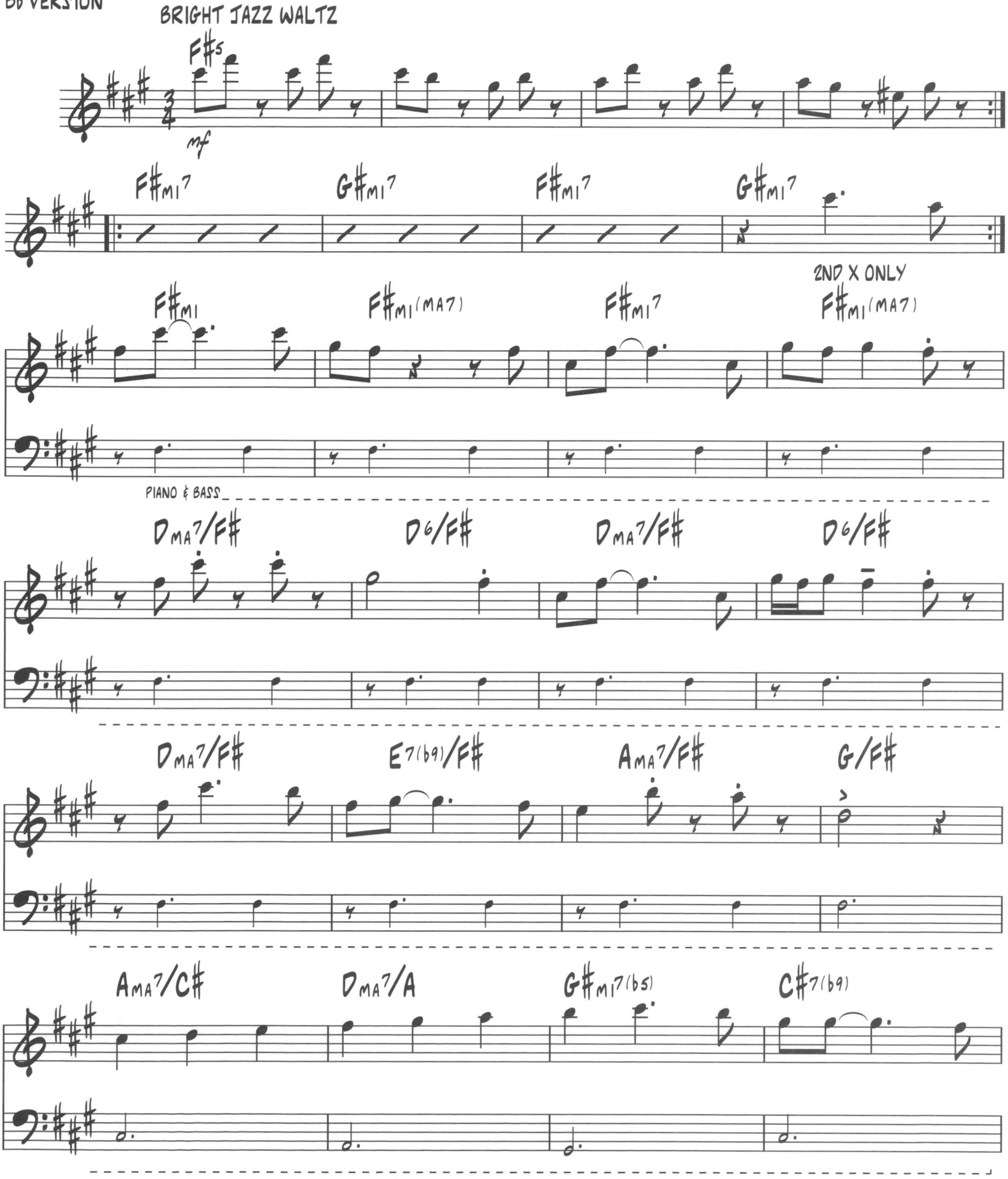
BRIGHT JAZZ WALTZ
F#5
mf
F#MI7
G#MI7
F#MI7
G#MI7
F#MI
F#MI(MA7)
F#MI7
2ND X ONLY
F#MI(MA7)
PIANO & BASS
DMA7/F#
D6/F#
DMA7/F#
D6/F#
DMA7/F#
E7(b9)/F#
AMA7/F#
G/F#
AMA7/C#
DMA7/A
G#MI7(b5)
C#7(b9)

F#MI7 G#MI7 F#MI7 G#MI7
F#MI7 G#MI7 F#MI7 G#MI7
SOLO (PLAY 12X'S)
F#MI7 G#MI7 F#MI7 G#MI7
LAST X ONLY
F#MI F#MI(MA7) F#MI7 F#MI(MA7)
DMA7/F# D6/F# DMA7/F# D6/F#
3
DMA7/F# E7(b9)/F# AMA7/F# G/F#
AMA7/C# DMA7/A G#MI7(b5) C#7(b9)
F#MA7 G#MI7 F#MA7 G#MI7
F#MA7 G#MI7 F#MA7 G#MI7
SOLO (PLAY 12X'S)
F#MA7 G#MI7 F#MA7 G#MI7
LAST X ONLY

F#MA7
G#MI7/F#
F#MA7
G#MI7/F#
BMA7/F#
C#MI7/F#
BMA7/F#
C#MI7/F#
DMA7/F#
E7(b9)/F#
AMA7/F#
G/F#
AMA7/C#
DMA7/A
G#MI7(b5)
C#7(b9)
F#MI7
G#MI7(b5)
C#7(b9)
F#MI7
DMA7
C#MI7
DMA7
C#MI7
F#MI7
B7
F#MI7
BMI7
E7(b9)
C#MI7
DMA7
C#MI7
DMA7
1ST X ONLY
SOLO
F#MI7
G#MI7
F#MI7
G#MI7
F#MI7

CD

3: SPLIT TRACK/MELODY

4: FULL STEREO TRACK

BUT NOT FOR ME

MUSIC AND LYRICS BY GEORGE GERSHWIN
AND IRA GERSHWIN

B♭ VERSION

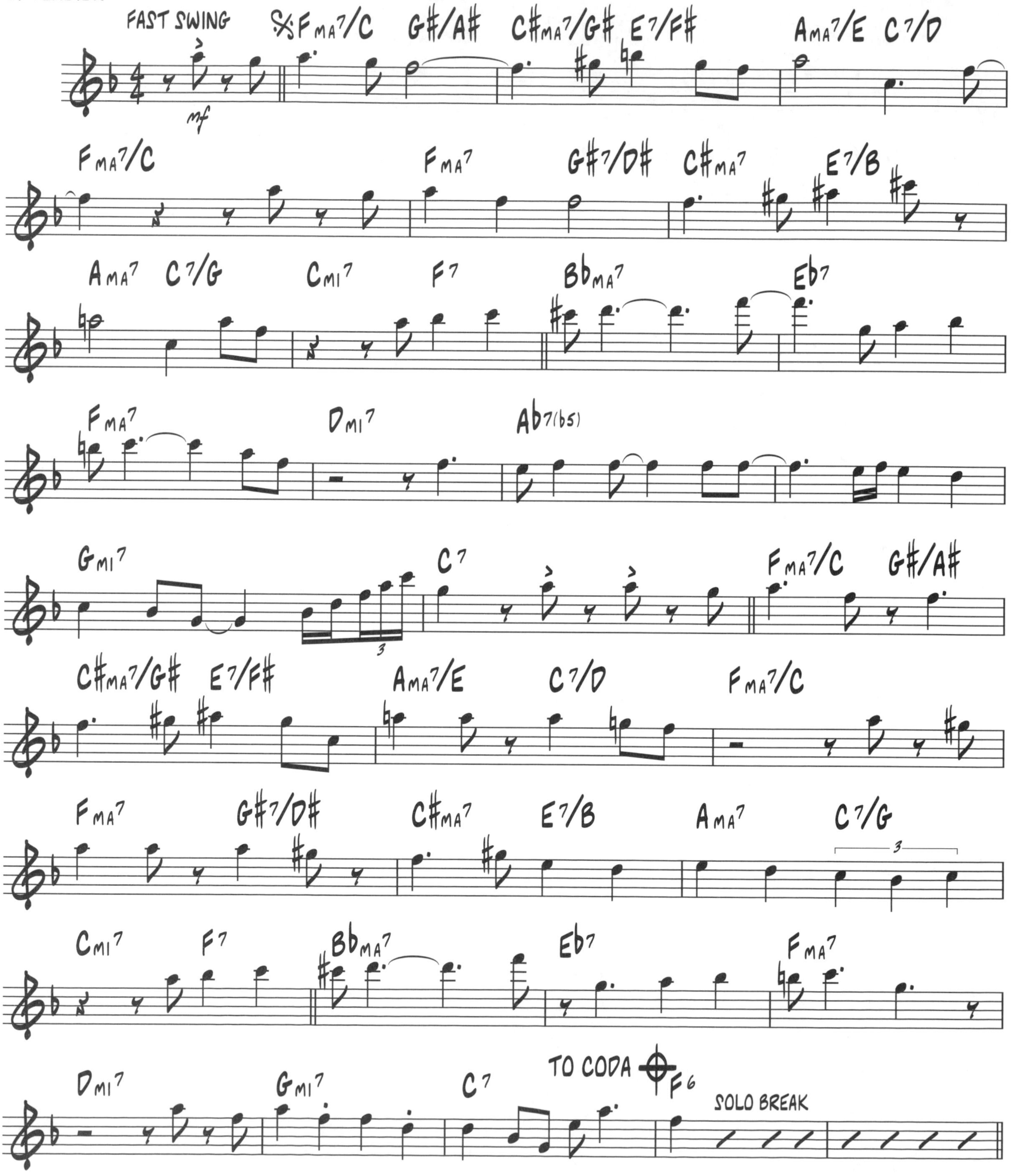

FAST SWING

FMA7/C G#/A# C#MA7/G# E7/F# AMA7/E C7/D

FMA7/C FMA7 G#7/D# C#MA7 E7/B

AMA7 C7/G CMI7 F7 B♭MA7 E♭7

FMA7 DMI7 A♭7(♭5)

GMI7 C7 FMA7/C G#/A#

C#MA7/G# E7/F# AMA7/E C7/D FMA7/C

FMA7 G#7/D# C#MA7 E7/B AMA7 C7/G

CMI7 F7 B♭MA7 E♭7 FMA7

DMI7 GMI7 C7 TO CODA F6 SOLO BREAK

SOLOS (2 CHORUSES)
FMA7/C G#/A# C#MA7/G# E7/F# AMA7/E C7/D FMA7/C
FMA7 G#7/D# C#MA7 E7/B AMA7 C7/G CMI7 F7
BbMA7 Eb7 FMA7 DMI7
Ab7(b5) GMI7 C7
FMA7/C G#/A# C#MA7/G# E7/F# AMA7/E C7/D FMA7/C
FMA7 G#7/D# C#MA7 E7/B AMA7 C7/G CMI7 F7
BbMA7 Eb7 FMA7 DMI7
GMI7 C7 F6
D.S. AL CODA
LAST X ONLY
CODA
N.C. BbMI7 Eb7 AMI7 D+7(#9)
PIANO
GMI7 C7SUS C7(b9) FMA7
3

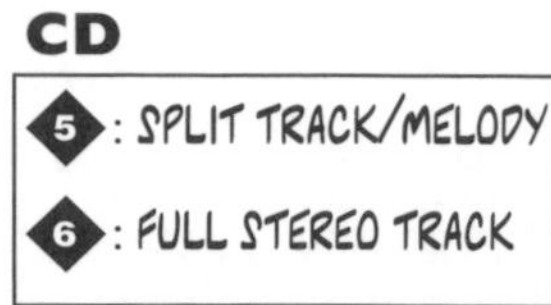

CD

5 : SPLIT TRACK/MELODY
6 : FULL STEREO TRACK

Bb VERSION

GREENSLEEVES

TRADITIONAL
ARRANGED BY McCOY TYNER

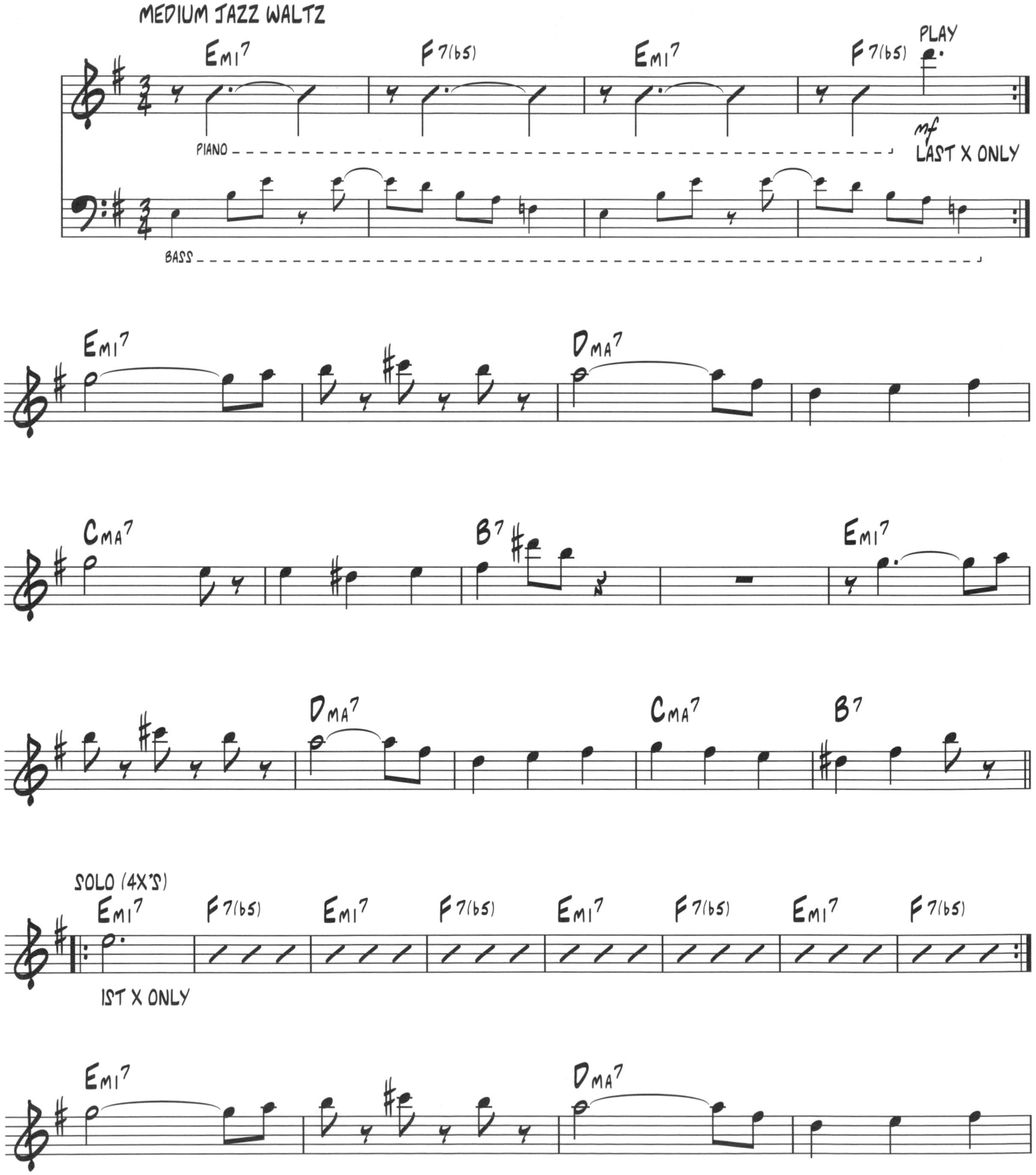
MEDIUM JAZZ WALTZ
EMI7
F7(b5)
EMI7
F7(b5)
PLAY
mf
LAST X ONLY
PIANO
BASS
EMI7
DMA7
CMA7
B7
EMI7
DMA7
CMA7
B7
SOLO (4X'S)
EMI7
F7(b5)
EMI7
F7(b5)
EMI7
F7(b5)
EMI7
F7(b5)
1ST X ONLY
EMI7
DMA7

CMA7
B7
EMI7
DMA7
CMA7
B7
SOLO (4X'S)
EMI7
F7(b5)
EMI7
F7(b5)
EMI7
F7(b5)
EMI7
F7(b5)
1ST X ONLY
EMI7
DMA7
CMA7
B7
EMI7
DMA7
CMA7
B7
SOLO (4X'S)
EMI7
F7(b5)
EMI7
F7(b5)
EMI7
PIANO
1ST X ONLY
BASS

CD
7: SPLIT TRACK/MELODY
8: FULL STEREO TRACK

Bb VERSION

IN A SENTIMENTAL MOOD

BY DUKE ELLINGTON

B6/D# D7(b9) C#MI7 F#7 BMA7 G#MI7

C#MI7 F#7 Bb7SUS Bb7(b9)

3 3

CMI7 FMI7

3

DMI7(b5) G7(b9) CMI7 C7 TO CODA

FMI7 Bb7(b9) Eb6 DMI7(b5) G7(b9)

SOLO

CMI CMI(MA7) CMI7 CMI6 FMI FMI(MA7)

FMI7 DMI7(b5) G7(b9) CMI /Bb AMI7(b5) AbMA7 GMI7 C7

1. 2. D.S. AL CODA

FMI7 Bb7(b9) Eb6 DMI7(b5) G7(b9) Eb6 C#MI7 F#7

CODA FMI7 Bb7(b9) Eb6 PIANO

CD
9 : SPLIT TRACK/MELODY
10 : FULL STEREO TRACK
LUSH LIFE
WORDS AND MUSIC BY
BILLY STRAYHORN
Bb VERSION
RUBATO
FASTER
SLOW
SLOW BALLAD

EbMA7 E7(b5) EbMA7 E7(b5) Eb6 Eb7 D7 GMA7 B+7
BbMA7 F+7(#9) BbMA7 F#MI7 B7 EMA7 EMI7 A7 DMA7 Bb7
EbMA7 E7(b5) EbMA7 E7(b5) Eb6 D7(#9)(b5) C#7
C7SUS C7(b9) G#MI7 C#7 B+7 Bb7 EbMA7 Ab7
TO CODA
GMI7 C7 G#MI7 C#7 B+7 Bb7
DBL. TIME FEEL
SOLO
Bb7(#9) B7(#9) C7(#9) C#7(#9) D7(#9) E7(b5) EbMA7 Bb7 EbMA7 E7(b5) EbMA7 E7(b5)
EbMA7 E7(b5) EbMA7 E7(b5) Eb6 G#MI7 C#7 F#MA7 F+7 E7(b5)
EbMA7 E7(b5) EbMA7 E7(b5) Eb6 Eb7 D7 GMA7
D.S. AL CODA
BbMA7 F+7(#9) BbMA7 F#MI7 B7 EMA7 EMI7 A7 DMA7 Bb7
CODA
Bb7(#9) B7(#9) C7(#9) C#7(#9) D7(#9) E7(b5) EbMA7

CD

13 : SPLIT TRACK/MELODY

14 : FULL STEREO TRACK

Bb VERSION

MY ONE AND ONLY LOVE

WORDS BY ROBERT MELLIN
MUSIC BY GUY WOOD

MEDIUM JAZZ BALLAD

DMA7 B7 EMI7 A7 F#7(b9)/A# BMI7 GMA7

mf

F#MI7 B7 EMI7 A7 F#7(b9)/A# BMI7 E7

EMI7 A7 F#MI7 B7 EMI7 A7 DMA7 B7

EMI7 A7 F#7(b9)/A# BMI7 GMA7 F#MI7 B7

EMI7 A7 F#7(b9) BMI7 E7 EMI7 A7

DMA7 G#MI7(b5) C#7(b9) 𝄋 F#MI7 G#MI7(b5) C#7(b9)

F#MI7 G#MI7(b5) C#7(b9) F#MI7 F#MI(MA7)/F

F#MI7/E
D#MI7(b5)
EMI7
A7(b9)
DMA7
B7
EMI7
A7
F#7(b9)/A#
BMI7
GMA7
F#MI7
B7
EMI7
A7
F#7(b9)/A#
BMI7
E7(b9)
EMI7
A7
TO CODA
DMA7/A
A7
SOLO
DMA7
IST X ONLY
B7
EMI7
A7
F#7(b9)/A#
BMI7
GMA7
F#MI7
B7
EMI7
A7
F#7(b9)/A#
BMI7
E7
EMI7
A7
1.
F#MI7
B7
EMI7
A7
2.
D.S. AL CODA
DMA7
G#MI7(b5)
C#7(b9)
CODA
DMA7/A
A7
DMA7

CD

MY SHINING HOUR

LYRIC BY JOHNNY MERCER
MUSIC BY HAROLD ARLEN

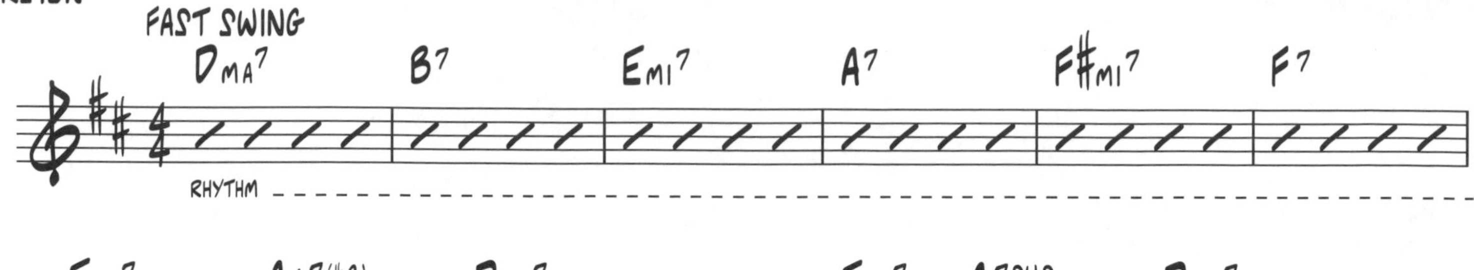

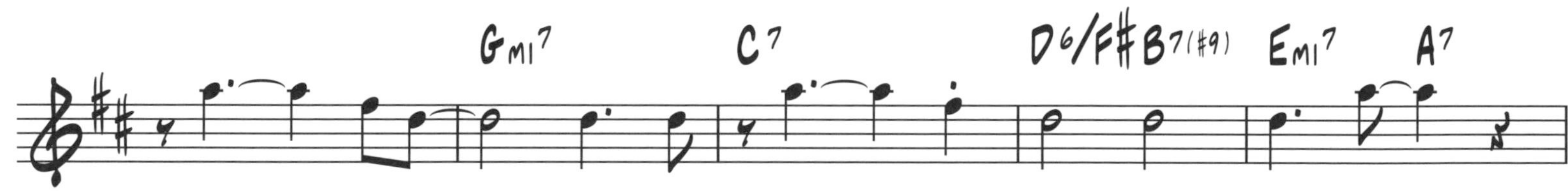

F#MI7 B7 EMI7 C#MI7(b5) F#7(b9) BMI7 C#MI7(b5)
F#7(b9) BMI7 E7(b5) EMI7 A7 AMI7 D7
GMA7 GMI7 C7 D6/F#B7 EMI7 A7 DMA7
EMI7 A7 DMA7 F#MI7B7 EMI7 A7 D6 EMI7 A7
DMA7 EMI7 A7SUS DMA7 EMI7 A7 DMA7EMI7 F#MI7 B7
EMI7 C#MI7(b5) F#7(b9) BMI7 C#MI7(b5) F#7(b9)
BMI7 E7 EMI7 A7 AMI7 D7
GMA7 GMI7 C7 D6/F#B7 EMI7 A7
DMA7 EMI7 A7 DMA7 F#MI7 B7 EMI7 A7
GMI7C7 F#MI7B7 EMI7 A7 D6 DMA7(b5)

CD

17 : SPLIT TRACK/MELODY
18 : FULL STEREO TRACK

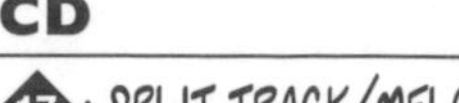

THE NIGHT HAS A THOUSAND EYES

WORDS BY BUDDY BERNIER
MUSIC BY JERRY BRAININ

B♭ VERSION

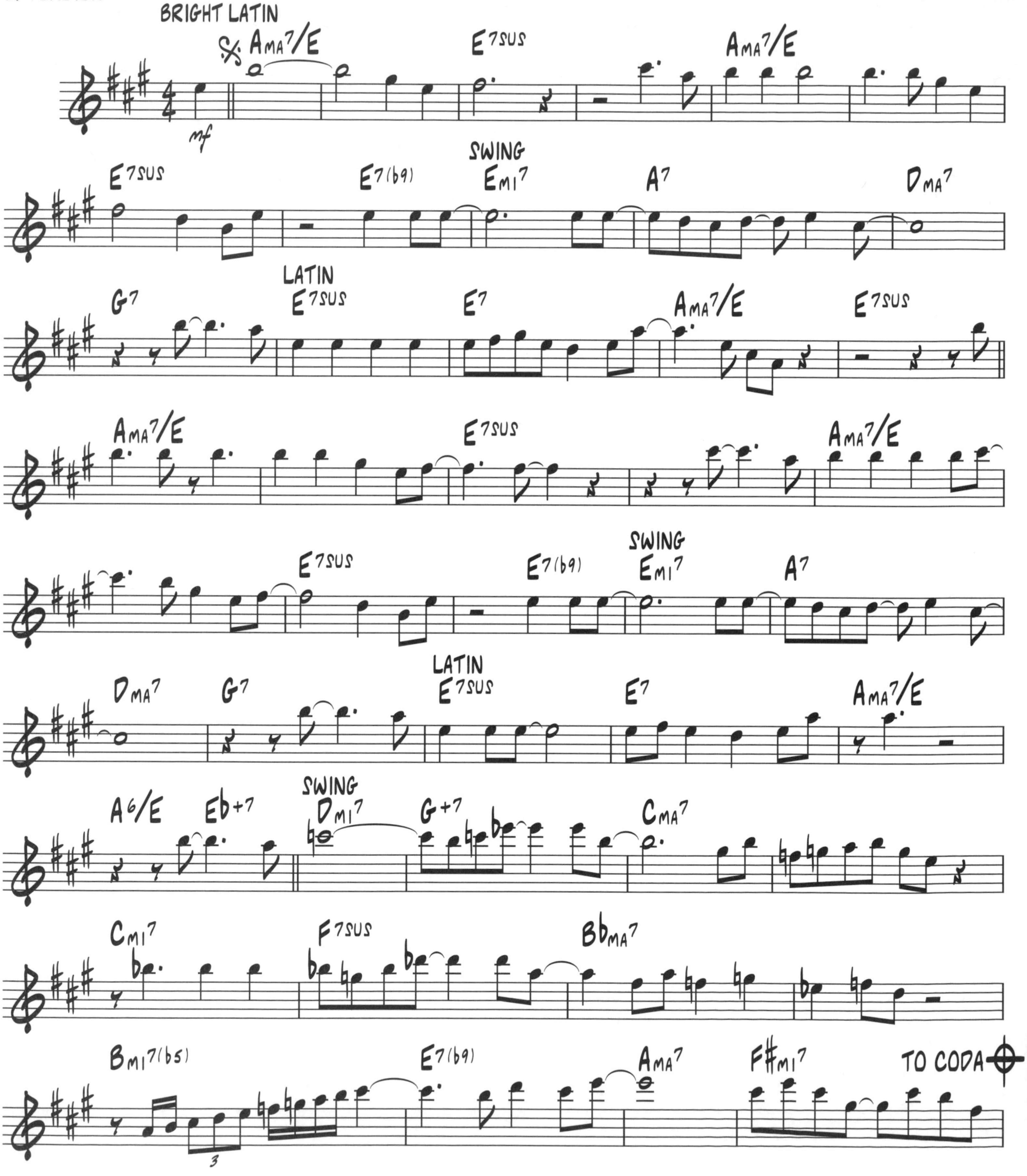

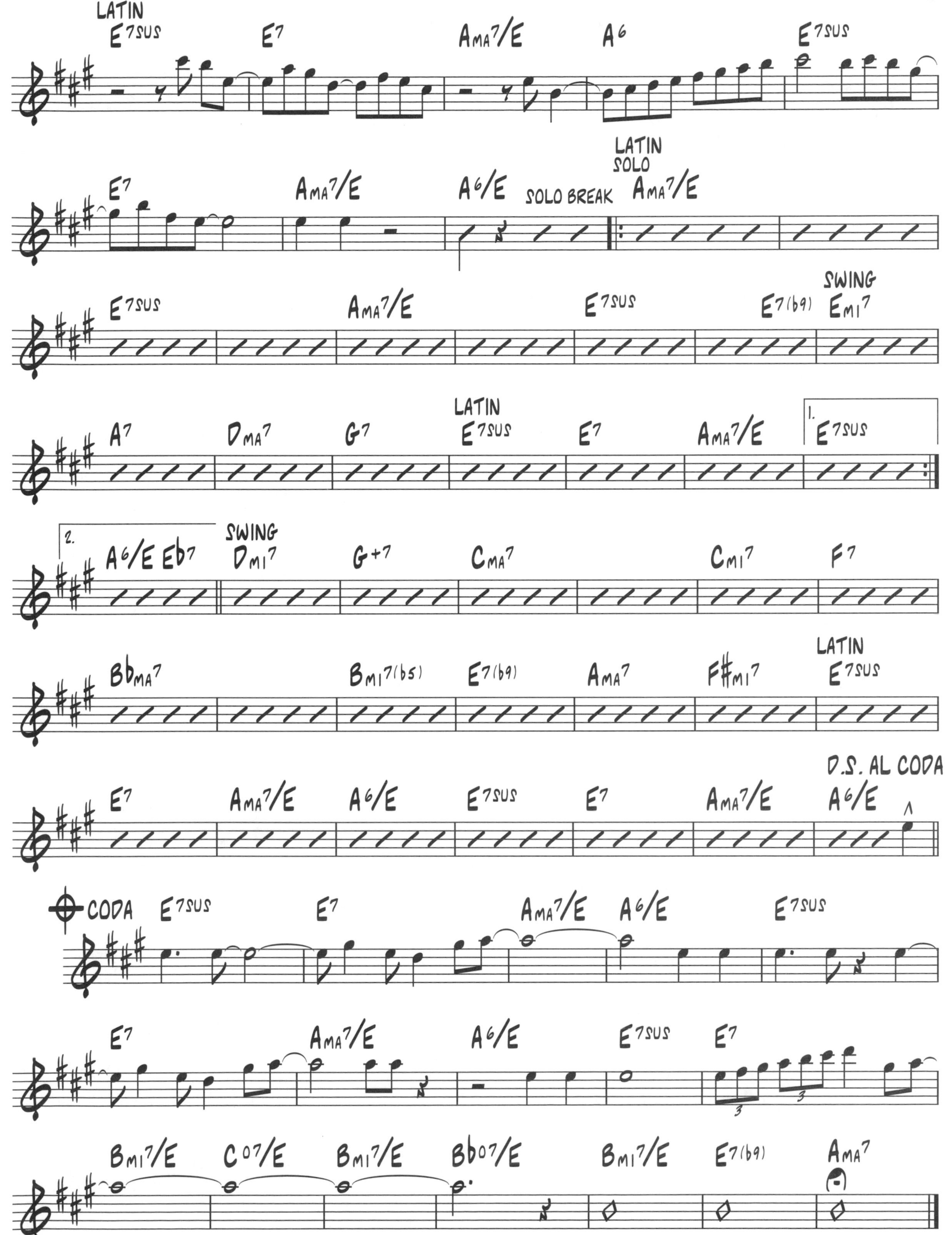
LATIN
E7SUS E7 AMA7/E A6 E7SUS
E7 AMA7/E A6/E SOLO BREAK
LATIN
SOLO
AMA7/E
E7SUS AMA7/E E7SUS E7(b9)
SWING
EMI7
A7 DMA7 G7
LATIN
E7SUS E7 AMA7/E
1.
E7SUS
2.
A6/E Eb7
SWING
DMI7 G+7 CMA7 CMI7 F7
BbMA7 BMI7(b5) E7(b9) AMA7 F#MI7
LATIN
E7SUS
E7 AMA7/E A6/E E7SUS E7 AMA7/E A6/E
D.S. AL CODA
CODA E7SUS E7 AMA7/E A6/E E7SUS
E7 AMA7/E A6/E E7SUS E7
3
3
BMI7/E C°7/E BMI7/E Bb°7/E BMI7/E E7(b9) AMA7

CD

19: SPLIT TRACK/MELODY
20: FULL STEREO TRACK

SOFTLY AS IN A MORNING SUNRISE

LYRICS BY OSCAR HAMMERSTEIN II
MUSIC BY SIGMUND ROMBERG

B♭ VERSION

MEDIUM SWING

Dmi7 /C Emi7(b5)/Bb A+7 Dmi7 F7 Emi7(b5) A+7

Dmi7 /C Emi7(b5)/Bb A+7 Dmi7 Eb7(b5) Emi7(b5) A+7(#9)

Dmi7 /C Emi7(b5)/Bb A+7 Dmi7 F7 Emi7(b5) A+7

Dmi7 /C Emi7(b5)/Bb A+7 Dmi7 Gmi7 C7

Fma7 F#o7

Gmi7 G#o7 A7 Emi7(b5) Bb7 A7(b9)

Dmi7 /C Emi7(b5)/Bb A+7 Dmi7 F7 Emi7(b5) A+7

TO CODA

Dmi7 /C Emi7(b5)/Bb A+7 Dmi7 Eb7(b5) Emi7(b5) A+7(#9) Dmi7

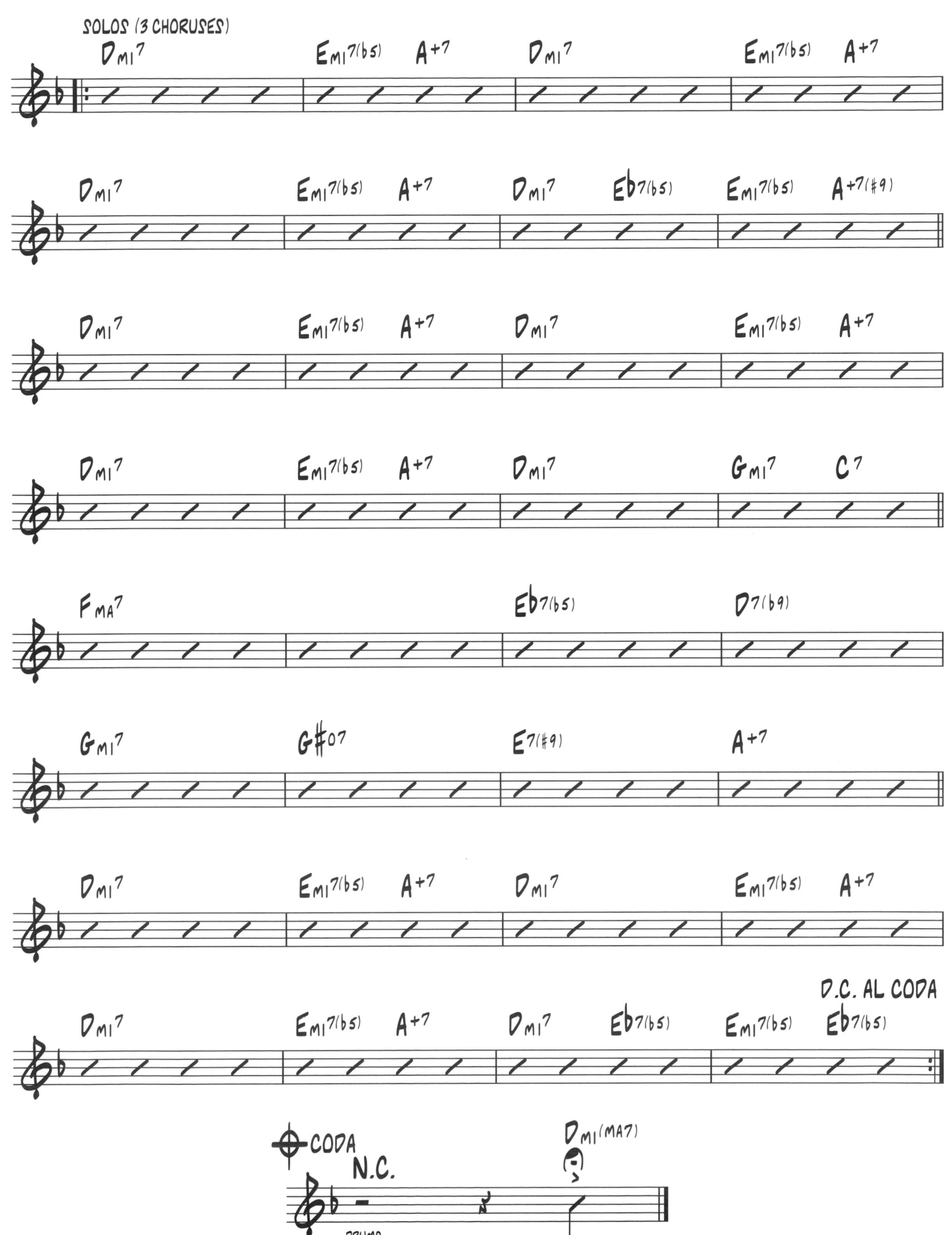
SOLOS (3 CHORUSES)
DMI7 EMI7(b5) A+7 DMI7 EMI7(b5) A+7
DMI7 EMI7(b5) A+7 DMI7 Eb7(b5) EMI7(b5) A+7(#9)
DMI7 EMI7(b5) A+7 DMI7 EMI7(b5) A+7
DMI7 EMI7(b5) A+7 DMI7 GMI7 C7
FMA7 Eb7(b5) D7(b9)
GMI7 G#O7 E7(#9) A+7
DMI7 EMI7(b5) A+7 DMI7 EMI7(b5) A+7
D.C. AL CODA
DMI7 EMI7(b5) A+7 DMI7 Eb7(b5) EMI7(b5) Eb7(b5)
CODA
N.C.
DMI(MA7)
DRUMS

CD
1: SPLIT TRACK/MELODY
2: FULL STEREO TRACK

ALL OR NOTHING AT ALL

WORDS BY JACK LAWRENCE
MUSIC BY ARTHUR ALTMAN

E♭ VERSION

BMI7/A
E7(b5)/A
AMA7
SWING
GMI7
C7
FMA7
GMI7
C7
GMI7
C7
GMI7
A7(b9)
DMI7
/C
Bb7
A7
G7(b5)
LATIN
F#MI(MA7)
F#MI6
F#MI(MA7)
F#MI6
F#MI(MA7)
F#MI6
G7
EMI7
BMI7
C#7(#9)
F#MI(MA7)
G7
A6
SWING
GMI7
C7
FMA7

GMI7
C7
GMI7
C7
GMI7
Bb7
A7(b5)
DMI7
/C
Bb7
A7
G7(b5)
LATIN
F#MI(MA7)
F#MI6
F#MI(MA7)
F#MI6
F#MI(MA7)
F#MI6
G7
EMI7
BMI7
C#7(#9)
F#MI(MA7)
G7
A6
G7
A6
G7
A6
G7
A6
G7
A6
G7
A6
G7
A6
G7
AMA7(b5)

CD
11 : SPLIT TRACK/MELODY
12 : FULL STEREO TRACK
MY FAVORITE THINGS
LYRICS BY OSCAR HAMMERSTEIN II
MUSIC BY RICHARD RODGERS
E♭ VERSION
BRIGHT JAZZ WALTZ
C♯5
mf
C♯MI7
D♯MI7
C♯MI7
D♯MI7
2ND X ONLY
C♯MI
C♯MI(MA7)
C♯MI7
C♯MI(MA7)
PIANO & BASS
AMA7/C♯
A6/C♯
AMA7/C♯
A6/C♯
AMA7/C♯
B7(♭9)/C♯
EMA7/C♯
D/C♯
EMA7/G♯
AMA7/E
D♯MI7(♭5)
G♯7(♭9)

C#MI7
D#MI7
SOLO (PLAY 12X'S)
LAST X ONLY
C#MI
C#MI(MA7)
AMA7/C#
A6/C#
B7(b9)/C#
EMA7/C#
D/C#
EMA7/G#
AMA7/E
D#MI7(b5)
G#7(b9)
C#MA7
SOLO (PLAY 12X'S)
LAST X ONLY

C#MA7
D#MI7/C#
C#MA7
D#MI7/C#
F#MA7/C#
G#MI7/C#
F#MA7/C#
G#MI7/C#
AMA7/C#
B7(b9)/C#
EMA7/C#
D/C#
EMA7/G#
AMA7/E
D#MI7(b5)
G#7(b9)
C#MI7
D#MI7(b5)
G#7(b9)
C#MI7
AMA7
G#MI7
AMA7
G#MI7
C#MI7
F#7
C#MI7
F#MI7
B7(b9)
G#MI7
AMA7
G#MI7
AMA7
1ST X ONLY
SOLO
C#MI7
D#MI7
C#MI7
D#MI7
C#MI7

CD

3 : SPLIT TRACK/MELODY

4 : FULL STEREO TRACK

BUT NOT FOR ME

MUSIC AND LYRICS BY GEORGE GERSHWIN
AND IRA GERSHWIN

Eb VERSION

SOLOS (2 CHORUSES)
CMA7/G D#/F G#MA7/D# B7/C# EMA7/B G7/A CMA7/G
CMA7 D#7/A# G#MA7 B7/F# EMA7 G7/D GMI7 C7
FMA7 Bb7 CMA7 AMI7
Eb7(b5) DMI7 G7
CMA7/G D#/F G#MA7/D# B7/C# EMA7/B G7/A CMA7/G
CMA7 D#7/A# G#MA7 B7/F# EMA7 G7/D GMI7 C7
FMA7 Bb7 CMA7 AMI7
DMI7 G7 C6
D.S. AL CODA
LAST X ONLY
CODA
N.C. FMI7 Bb7 EMI7 A+7(#9)
PIANO
DMI7 G7SUS G7(b9) CMA7

CD

5 : SPLIT TRACK/MELODY

6 : FULL STEREO TRACK

Eb VERSION

GREENSLEEVES

TRADITIONAL
ARRANGED BY McCOY TYNER

GMA7
F#7
BMI7
AMA7
GMA7
F#7
SOLO (4X'S)
BMI7
C7(b5)
BMI7
C7(b5)
BMI7
C7(b5)
BMI7
C7(b5)
1ST X ONLY
BMI7
AMA7
GMA7
F#7
BMI7
AMA7
GMA7
F#7
SOLO (4X'S)
BMI7
C7(b5)
BMI7
C7(b5)
BMI7
PIANO
1ST X ONLY
BASS

CD

7: SPLIT TRACK/MELODY

8: FULL STEREO TRACK

Eb VERSION

IN A SENTIMENTAL MOOD

BY DUKE ELLINGTON

F#6/A# A7(b9) G#MI7 C#7 F#MA7 D#MI7
G#MI7 C#7 F7SUS F7(b9)
GMI7 CMI7
AMI7(b5) D7(b9) GMI7 G7 TO CODA
CMI7 F7(b9) Bb6 AMI7(b5) D7(b9)
SOLO
GMI7 GMI(MA7) GMI7 GMI6 CMI CMI(MA7)
CMI7 AMI7(b5) D7(b9) GMI /F EMI7(b5) EbMA7 DMI7 G7
CMI7 F7(b9) 1. Bb6 AMI7(b5) D7(b9) 2. Bb6 G#MI7 C#7 D.S. AL CODA
CODA CMI7 F7(b9) Bb6 PIANO

CD

LUSH LIFE

WORDS AND MUSIC BY
BILLY STRAYHORN

Eb VERSION

RUBATO

F7(#9) | Bb6 Ab7 | Bbma7 Ab7 | Bbma7 Ab7

Bbma7 Cmi7 Dmi7 D#mi7 | Fmi7 B7 | Cmi7 F7(b5) B7

Bb6 B7(b5) | Bb6 Ab7 | Bb6 Ab7 | Bb6 Ab7

Bbma7 Cmi7 Dmi7 D#mi7 | Fmi7 B7(b5) | Cmi7 F+7

Bb6 Emi7(b5) A7(b9) | FASTER Dmi | Dmi6 | Dmi | Dmi7

Dmi | Emi7(b5) A7(b9) | Dmi | Dmi6 | Dmi | Dmi7

Dmi A7(b9)/C# | SLOW Cmi7 F7 | G#7(b5) G7 | Cmi7

F#7(b5) | Cmi7 | B7(b5)

SLOW BALLAD

Bbma7 B7(b5) | Bbma7 B7(b5) | Bb6 D#mi7 G#7 | C#ma7 C+7 B7(b5)

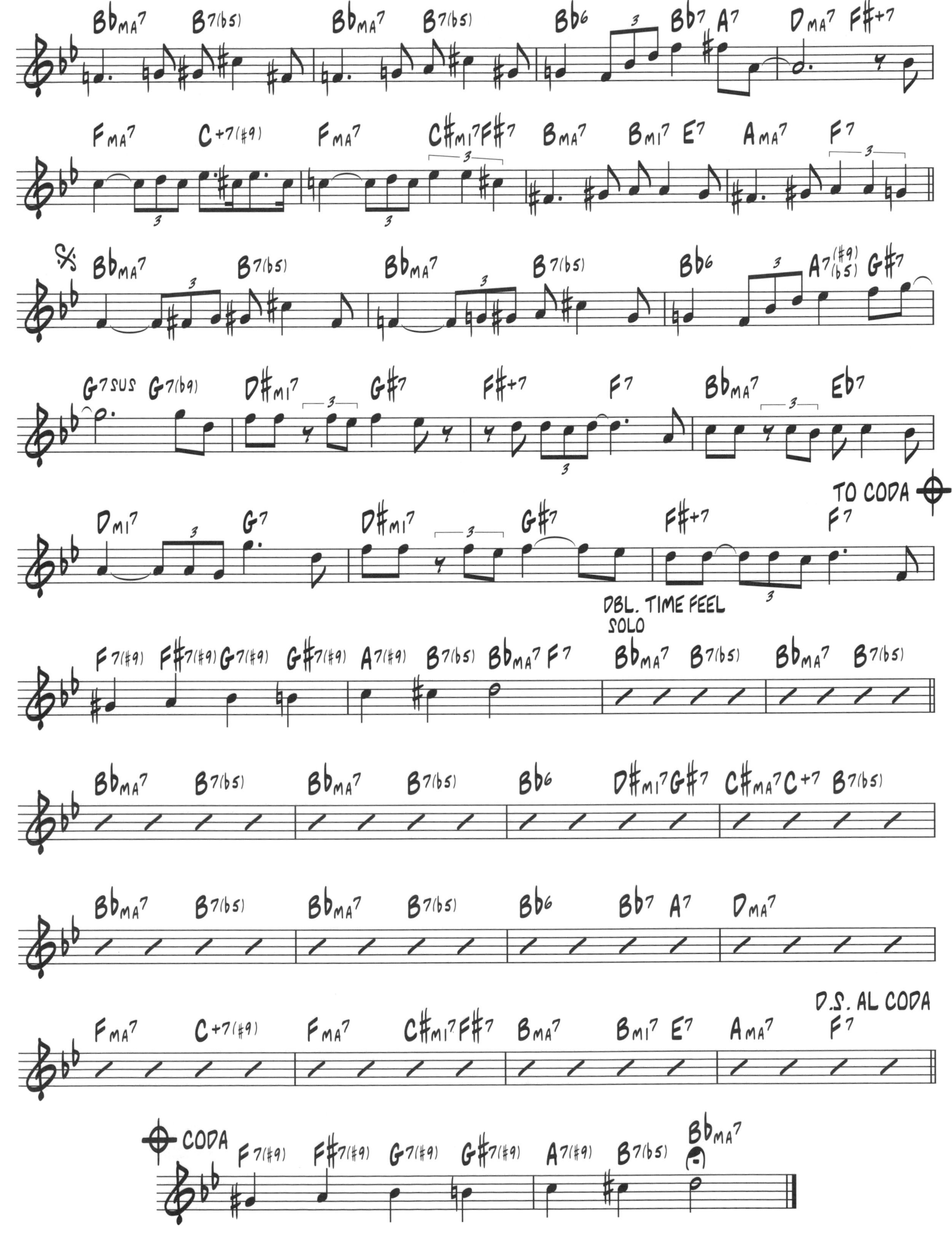
BbMA7 B7(b5) BbMA7 B7(b5) Bb6 Bb7 A7 DMA7 F#+7
FMA7 C+7(#9) FMA7 C#MI7 F#7 BMA7 BMI7 E7 AMA7 F7
BbMA7 B7(b5) BbMA7 B7(b5) Bb6 A7(#9)(b5) G#7
G7SUS G7(b9) D#MI7 G#7 F#+7 F7 BbMA7 Eb7
TO CODA
DMI7 G7 D#MI7 G#7 F#+7 F7
DBL. TIME FEEL
SOLO
F7(#9) F#7(#9) G7(#9) G#7(#9) A7(#9) B7(b5) BbMA7 F7 BbMA7 B7(b5) BbMA7 B7(b5)
BbMA7 B7(b5) BbMA7 B7(b5) Bb6 D#MI7 G#7 C#MA7 C+7 B7(b5)
BbMA7 B7(b5) BbMA7 B7(b5) Bb6 Bb7 A7 DMA7
D.S. AL CODA
FMA7 C+7(#9) FMA7 C#MI7 F#7 BMA7 BMI7 E7 AMA7 F7
CODA
F7(#9) F#7(#9) G7(#9) G#7(#9) A7(#9) B7(b5) BbMA7

CD

13: SPLIT TRACK/MELODY

14: FULL STEREO TRACK

MY ONE AND ONLY LOVE

WORDS BY ROBERT MELLIN
MUSIC BY GUY WOOD

E♭ VERSION

MEDIUM JAZZ BALLAD

AMA7 F♯7 BMI7 E7 C♯7(♭9)/F F♯MI7 DMA7

C♯MI7 F♯7 BMI7 E7 C♯7(♭9)/F F♯MI7 B7

BMI7 E7 C♯MI7 F♯7 BMI7 E7 AMA7 F♯7

BMI7 E7 C♯7(♭9)/F F♯MI7 DMA7 C♯MI7 F♯7

BMI7 E7 C♯7(♭9) F♯MI7 B7 BMI7 E7

AMA7 D♯MI7(♭5) G♯7(♭9) C♯MI7 D♯MI7(♭5) G♯7(♭9)

C♯MI7 D♯MI7(♭5) G♯7(♭9) C♯MI7 C♯MI(MA7)/C

C#MI7/B
A#MI7(b5)
BMI7
E7(b9)
AMA7
F#7
BMI7
E7
C#7(b9)/F
F#MI7
DMA7
C#MI7
F#7
BMI7
E7
C#7(b9)/F
F#MI7
B7(b9)
BMI7
E7
TO CODA
AMA7/E
E7
SOLO
AMA7
1ST X ONLY
F#7
BMI7
E7
C#7(b9)/F
F#MI7
DMA7
C#MI7
F#7
BMI7
E7
C#7(b9)/F
F#MI7
B7
BMI7
E7
1.
C#MI7
F#7
BMI7
E7
2.
D.S. AL CODA
AMA7
D#MI7(b5)
G#7(b9)
CODA
AMA7/E
E7
AMA7

CD

15: SPLIT TRACK/MELODY

16: FULL STEREO TRACK

Eb VERSION

MY SHINING HOUR

LYRIC BY JOHNNY MERCER
MUSIC BY HAROLD ARLEN

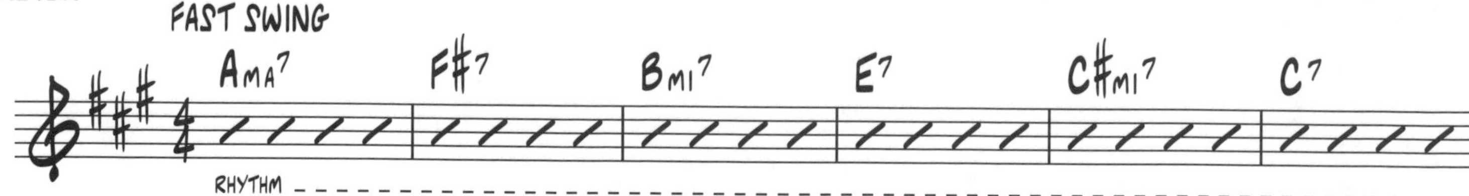

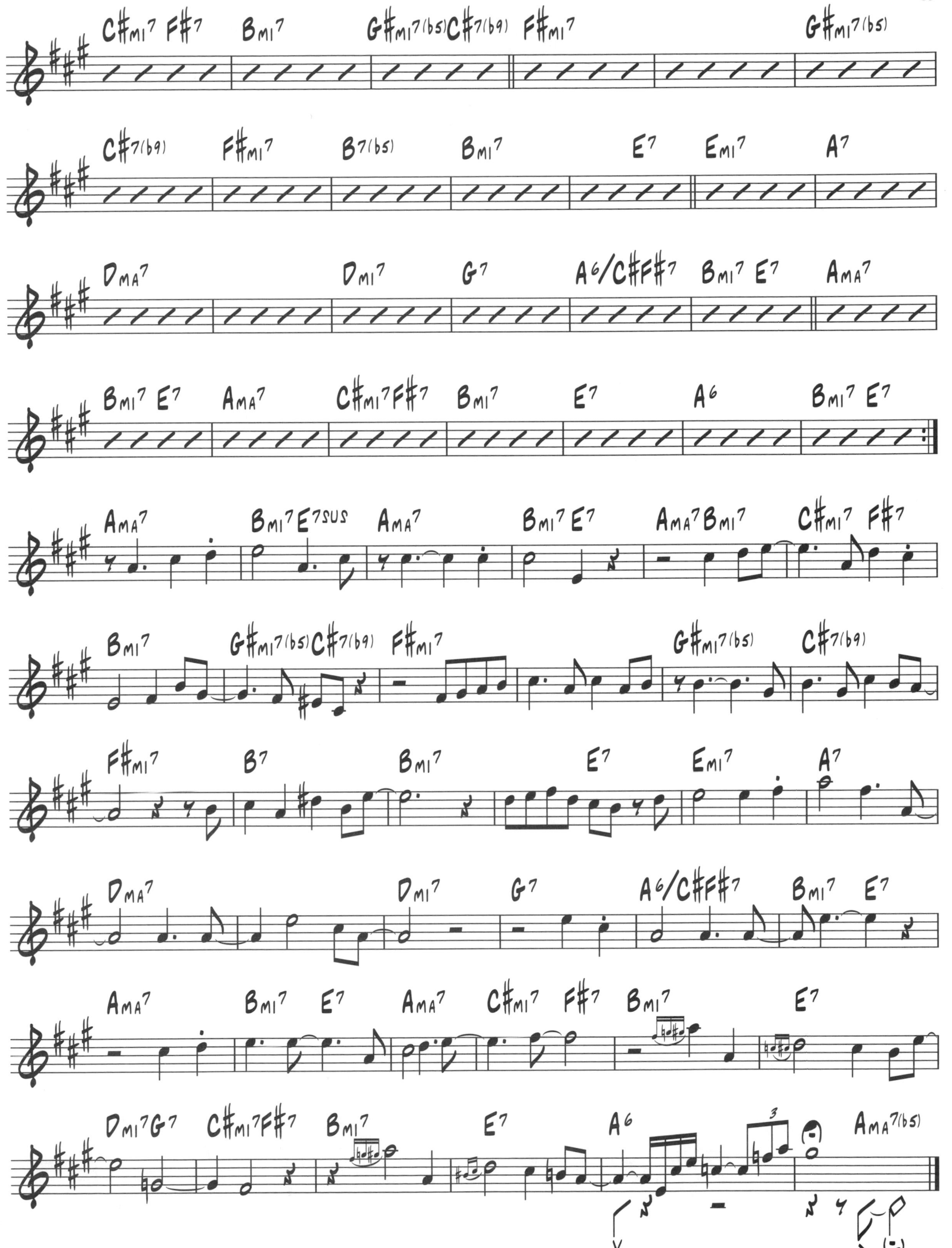

C#MI7 F#7 BMI7 G#MI7(b5) C#7(b9) F#MI7 G#MI7(b5)
C#7(b9) F#MI7 B7(b5) BMI7 E7 EMI7 A7
DMA7 DMI7 G7 A6/C# F#7 BMI7 E7 AMA7
BMI7 E7 AMA7 C#MI7 F#7 BMI7 E7 A6 BMI7 E7
AMA7 BMI7 E7SUS AMA7 BMI7 E7 AMA7 BMI7 C#MI7 F#7
BMI7 G#MI7(b5) C#7(b9) F#MI7 G#MI7(b5) C#7(b9)
F#MI7 B7 BMI7 E7 EMI7 A7
DMA7 DMI7 G7 A6/C# F#7 BMI7 E7
AMA7 BMI7 E7 AMA7 C#MI7 F#7 BMI7 E7
DMI7 G7 C#MI7 F#7 BMI7 E7 A6 3 AMA7(b5)

CD
17 : SPLIT TRACK/MELODY
18 : FULL STEREO TRACK

THE NIGHT HAS A THOUSAND EYES

WORDS BY BUDDY BERNIER
MUSIC BY JERRY BRAININ

Eb VERSION

LATIN
B7SUS
B7
EMA7/B
E6
B7SUS
B7
EMA7/B
E6/B
SOLO BREAK
LATIN
SOLO
EMA7/B
B7SUS
EMA7/B
B7SUS
B7(b9)
SWING
BMI7
E7
AMA7
D7
LATIN
B7SUS
B7
EMA7/B
1.
B7SUS
2.
E6/B Bb7
SWING
AMI7
D+7
GMA7
GMI7
C7
FMA7
F#MI7(b5)
B7(b9)
EMA7
C#MI7
LATIN
B7SUS
B7
EMA7/B
E6/B
B7SUS
B7
EMA7/B
D.S. AL CODA
E6/B
CODA
B7SUS
B7
EMA7/B
E6/B
B7SUS
B7
EMA7/B
E6/B
B7SUS
B7
F#MI7/B
G°7/B
F#MI7/B
F°7/B
F#MI7/B
B7(b9)
EMA7

CD

19: SPLIT TRACK/MELODY

20: FULL STEREO TRACK

SOFTLY AS IN A MORNING SUNRISE

LYRICS BY OSCAR HAMMERSTEIN II
MUSIC BY SIGMUND ROMBERG

SOLOS (3 CHORUSES)
AMI7
BMI7(b5) E+7
AMI7
BMI7(b5) E+7
AMI7
BMI7(b5) E+7
AMI7 Bb7(b5)
BMI7(b5) E+7(#9)
AMI7
BMI7(b5) E+7
AMI7
BMI7(b5) E+7
AMI7
BMI7(b5) E+7
AMI7
DMI7 G7
CMA7
Bb7(b5)
A7(b9)
DMI7
D#07
B7(#9)
E+7
AMI7
BMI7(b5) E+7
AMI7
BMI7(b5) E+7
D.C. AL CODA
AMI7
BMI7(b5) E+7
AMI7 Bb7(b5)
BMI7(b5) Bb7(b5)
CODA
N.C.
AMI(MA7)
DRUMS

ALL OR NOTHING AT ALL

WORDS BY JACK LAWRENCE
MUSIC BY ARTHUR ALTMAN

SWING
LATIN
SWING

Bbmi7
Eb7
Bbmi7
Eb7
Bbmi7
Db7
C7(b5)
Fmi7
/Eb
Db7
C7
Bb7(b5)
LATIN
Ami(MA7)
Ami6
Ami(MA7)
Ami6
Ami(MA7)
Ami6
Bb7
Gmi7
Dmi7
E7(#9)
Ami(MA7)
Bb7
C6
Bb7
C6
Bb7
C6
Bb7
C6
Bb7
C6
Bb7
C6
Bb7
C6
Bb7
Cma7(b5)

MY FAVORITE THINGS

EMI7
F#MI7
EMI7
F#MI7
EMI7
F#MI7
EMI7
F#MI7
SOLO (PLAY 12X'S)
EMI7
F#MI7
EMI7
F#MI7
LAST X ONLY
EMI
EMI(MA7)
EMI7
EMI(MA7)
CMA7/E
C6/E
CMA7/E
C6/E
3
CMA7/E
D7(b9)/E
GMA7/E
F/E
GMA7/B
CMA7/G
F#MI7(b5)
B7(b9)
EMA7
F#MI7
EMA7
F#MI7
EMA7
F#MI7
EMA7
F#MI7
SOLO (PLAY 12X'S)
EMA7
F#MI7
EMA7
F#MI7
LAST X ONLY

EMA7
F#MI7/E
EMA7
F#MI7/E
AMA7/E
BMI7/E
AMA7/E
BMI7/E
CMA7/E
D7(b9)/E
GMA7/E
F/E
GMA7/B
CMA7/G
F#MI7(b5)
B7(b9)
EMI7
F#MI7(b5)
B7(b9)
EMI7
CMA7
BMI7
CMA7
BMI7
EMI7
A7
EMI7
AMI7
D7(b9)
BMI7
CMA7
BMI7
CMA7
1ST X ONLY
SOLO
EMI7
F#MI7
EMI7
F#MI7
EMI7

CD

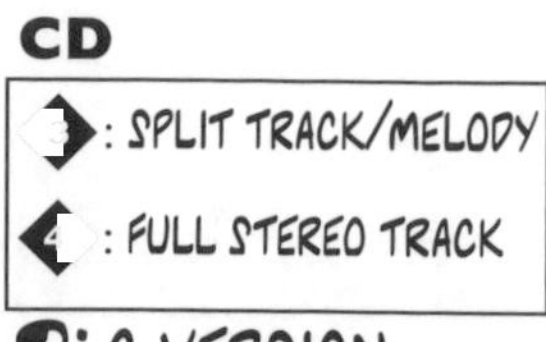

C VERSION

BUT NOT FOR ME

MUSIC AND LYRICS BY GEORGE GERSHWIN
AND IRA GERSHWIN

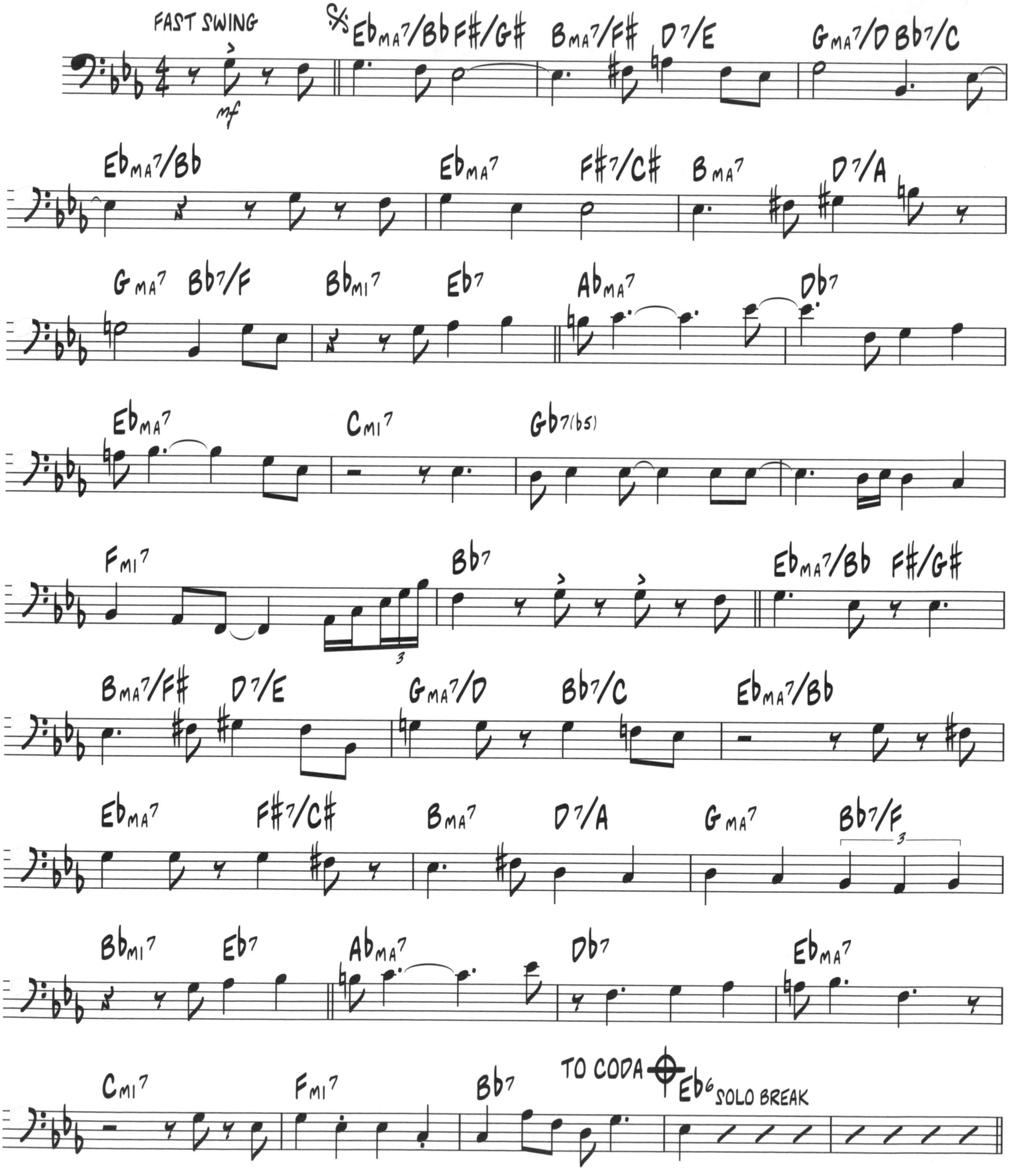

FAST SWING

Ebma7/Bb F#/G# Bma7/F# D7/E Gma7/D Bb7/C

Ebma7/Bb Ebma7 F#7/C# Bma7 D7/A

Gma7 Bb7/F Bbmi7 Eb7 Abma7 Db7

Ebma7 Cmi7 Gb7(b5)

Fmi7 Bb7 Ebma7/Bb F#/G#

Bma7/F# D7/E Gma7/D Bb7/C Ebma7/Bb

Ebma7 F#7/C# Bma7 D7/A Gma7 Bb7/F

Bbmi7 Eb7 Abma7 Db7 Ebma7

Cmi7 Fmi7 Bb7 TO CODA Eb6 SOLO BREAK

SOLOS (2 CHORUSES)
Ebma7/Bb F#/G# Bma7/F# D7/E Gma7/D Bb7/C Ebma7/Bb
Ebma7 F#7/C# Bma7 D7/A Gma7 Bb7/F Bbmi7 Eb7
Abma7 Db7 Ebma7 Cmi7
Gb7(b5) Fmi7 Bb7
Ebma7/Bb F#/G# Bma7/F# D7/E Gma7/D Bb7/C Ebma7/Bb
Ebma7 F#7/C# Bma7 D7/A Gma7 Bb7/F Bbmi7 Eb7
Abma7 Db7 Ebma7 Cmi7
Fmi7 Bb7 Eb6 D.S. AL CODA
LAST X ONLY
CODA
N.C. Abmi7 Db7 Gmi7 C+7(#9)
PIANO
Fmi7 Bb7SUS Bb7(b9) Ebma7
3

GREENSLEEVES

TRADITIONAL
ARRANGED BY McCOY TYNER

C VERSION

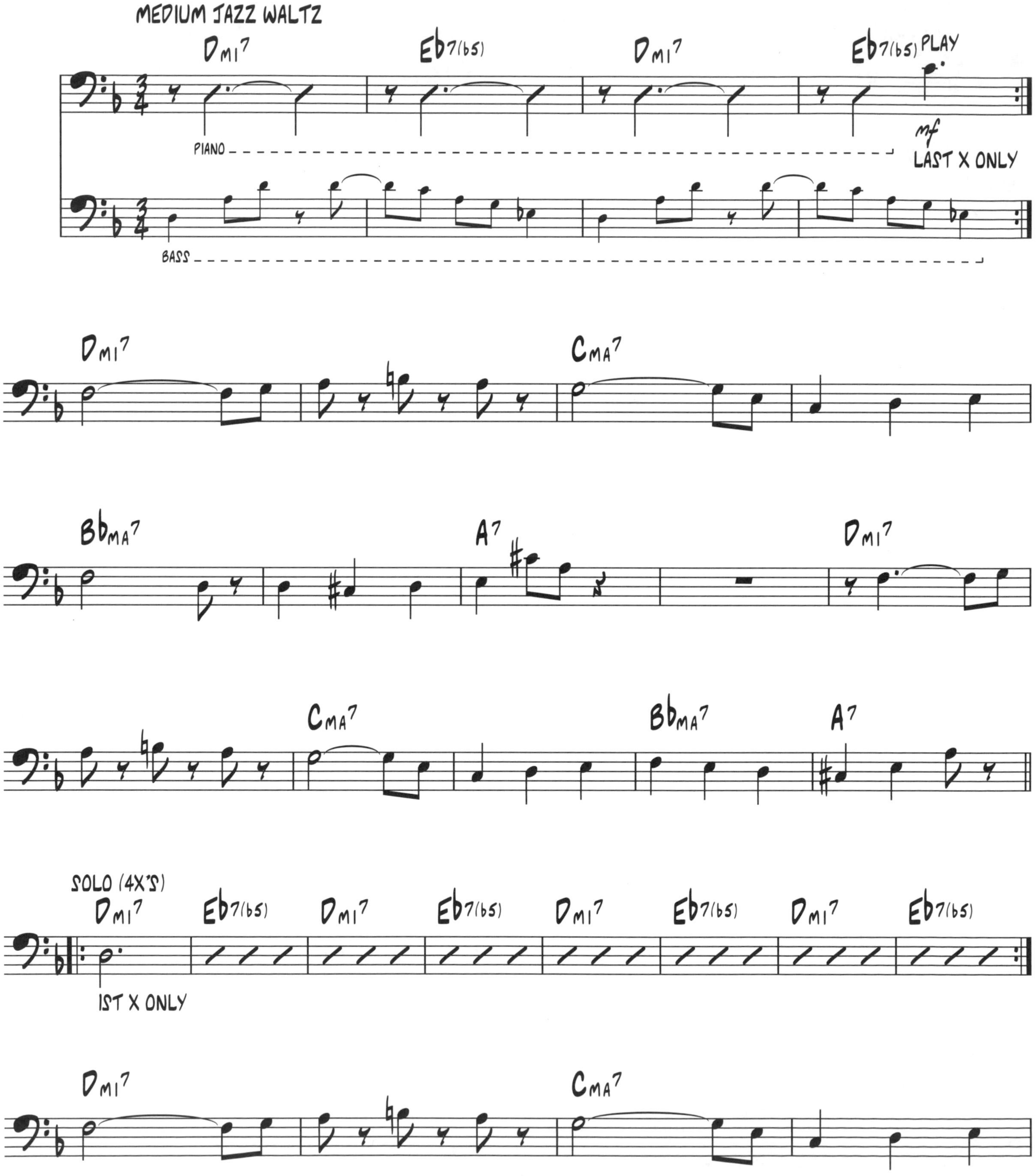

Dmi7 Cma7

Bbma7 A7 Dmi7

Cma7 Bbma7 A7

BbMA7
A7
DMI7
CMA7
BbMA7
A7
SOLO (4X'S)
DMI7
Eb7(b5)
DMI7
Eb7(b5)
DMI7
Eb7(b5)
DMI7
Eb7(b5)
1ST X ONLY
DMI7
CMA7
BbMA7
A7
DMI7
CMA7
BbMA7
A7
SOLO (4X'S)
DMI7
Eb7(b5)
DMI7
Eb7(b5)
DMI7
PIANO
1ST X ONLY
BASS

CD

7 : SPLIT TRACK/MELODY
8 : FULL STEREO TRACK

𝄢: C VERSION

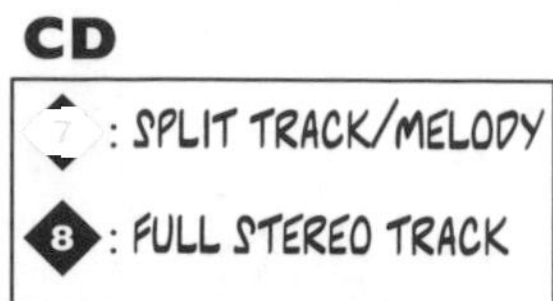

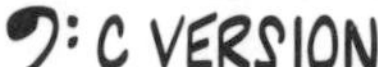

IN A SENTIMENTAL MOOD

BY DUKE ELLINGTON

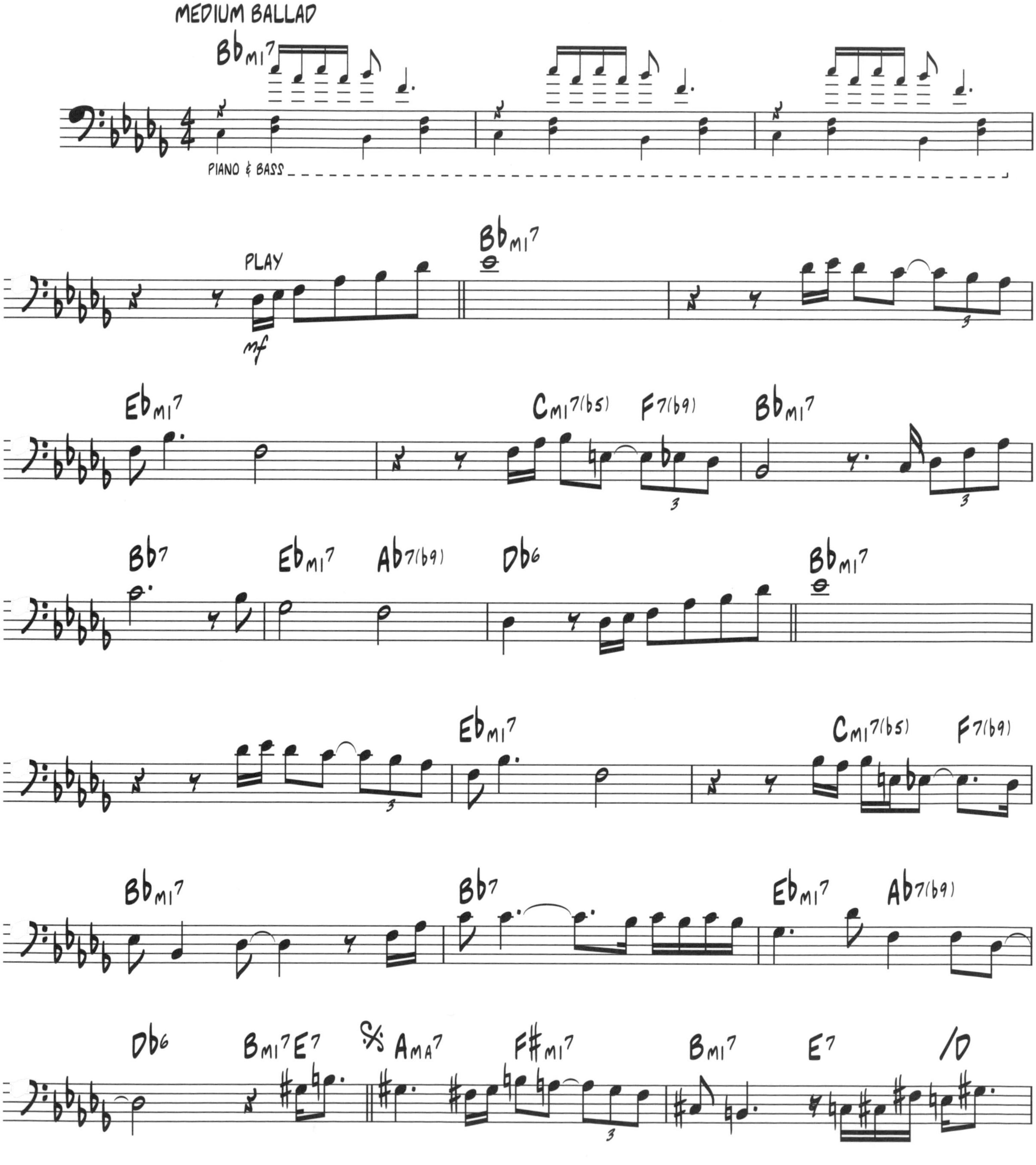
MEDIUM BALLAD
Bbmi7
PIANO & BASS
PLAY
mf
Bbmi7
Ebmi7
Cmi7(b5)
F7(b9)
Bbmi7
Bb7
Ebmi7
Ab7(b9)
Db6
Bbmi7
Ebmi7
Cmi7(b5)
F7(b9)
Bbmi7
Bb7
Ebmi7
Ab7(b9)
Db6
Bmi7 E7
Ama7
F#mi7
Bmi7
E7
/D

A6/C# C7(b9) Bmi7 E7 Ama7 F#mi7
Bmi7 E7 Ab7sus Ab7(b9)
3
3
Bbmi7 Ebmi7
3
Cmi7(b5) F7(b9) Bbmi7 Bb7
TO CODA
Ebmi7 Ab7(b9) Db6 Cmi7(b5) F7(b9)
SOLO
Bbmi Bbmi(ma7) Bbmi7 Bbmi6 Ebmi Ebmi(ma7)
Ebmi7 Cmi7(b5) F7(b9) Bbmi /Ab Gmi7(b5) Gbma7 Fmi7 Bb7
1.
2.
D.S. AL CODA
Ebmi7 Ab7(b9) Db6 Cmi7(b5) F7(b9) Db6 Bmi7 E7
CODA
Ebmi7 Ab7(b9) Db6
PIANO

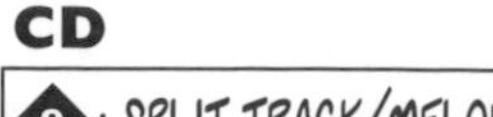

LUSH LIFE

WORDS AND MUSIC BY
BILLY STRAYHORN

C VERSION

RUBATO

Ab7(#9) | Db6 Cb7 | DbMA7 Cb7 | DbMA7 Cb7

DbMA7 EbMI7 FMI7 F#MI7 | AbMI7 D7 | EbMI7 Ab7(b5) D7

Db6 D7(b5) | Db6 Cb7 | Db6 Cb7 | Db6 Cb7

DbMA7 EbMI7 FMI7 F#MI7 | AbMI7 D7(b5) | EbMI7 Ab+7

Db6 GMI7(b5) C7(b9) | FASTER FMI FMI6 | FMI FMI7

FMI | GMI7(b5) C7(b9) | FMI FMI6 | FMI FMI7

FMI | SLOW C7(b9)/E EbMI7 Ab7 | B7(b5) | Bb7 | EbMI7

A7(b5) | EbMI7 D7(b5)

SLOW BALLAD

DbMA7 D7(b5) | DbMA7 D7(b5) | Db6 F#MI7 B7 | EMA7 Eb+7 D7(b5)

Db MA7 D7(b5) Db MA7 D7(b5) Db6 Db7 C7 F MA7 A+7

Ab MA7 Eb+7(#9) Ab MA7 E MI7 A7 D MA7 D MI7 G7 C MA7 Ab7

Db MA7 D7(b5) Db MA7 D7(b5) Db6 C7(#9/b5) B7

Bb7SUS Bb7(b9) F# MI7 B7 A+7 Ab7 Db MA7 Gb7

TO CODA

F MI7 Bb7 F# MI7 B7 A+7 Ab7

DBL. TIME FEEL
SOLO

Ab7(#9) A7(#9) Bb7(#9) B7(#9) C7(#9) D7(b5) Db MA7 Ab7 Db MA7 D7(b5) Db MA7 D7(b5)

Db MA7 D7(b5) Db MA7 D7(b5) Db6 F# MI7 B7 E MA7 Eb+7 D7(b5)

Db MA7 D7(b5) Db MA7 D7(b5) Db6 Db7 C7 F MA7

D.S. AL CODA

Ab MA7 Eb+7(#9) Ab MA7 E MI7 A7 D MA7 D MI7 G7 C MA7 Ab7

CODA

Ab7(#9) A7(#9) Bb7(#9) B7(#9) C7(#9) D7(b5) Db MA7

CD

13 : SPLIT TRACK/MELODY

14 : FULL STEREO TRACK

MY ONE AND ONLY LOVE

WORDS BY ROBERT MELLIN
MUSIC BY GUY WOOD

EMI7/D
C#MI7(b5)
DMI7
G7(b9)
CMA7
A7
DMI7
G7
E7(b9)/G#
AMI7
FMA7
EMI7
A7
DMI7
G7
E7(b9)/G#
AMI7
D7(b9)
DMI7
G7
TO CODA
CMA7/G
G7
SOLO
CMA7
1ST X ONLY
A7
DMI7
G7
E7(b9)/G#
AMI7
FMA7
EMI7
A7
DMI7
G7
E7(b9)/G#
AMI7
D7
DMI7
G7
1.
EMI7
A7
DMI7
G7
2.
D.S. AL CODA
CMA7
F#MI7(b5)
B7(b9)
CODA
CMA7/G
G7
CMA7

CD

15: SPLIT TRACK/MELODY
16: FULL STEREO TRACK

MY SHINING HOUR

LYRIC BY JOHNNY MERCER
MUSIC BY HAROLD ARLEN

C VERSION

FAST SWING

CMA7 A7 DMI7 G7 EMI7 Eb7

RHYTHM

DMI7 G+7(#9) CMA7 DMI7 G7SUS CMA7

DMI7 G7 CMA7 DMI7 EMI7 A7 DMI7 BMI7(b5) E7(b9)

AMI7 BMI7(b5) E7(b9) AMI7

D7 DMI7 G7 GMI7 C7 FMA7

FMI7 Bb7 C6/E A7(#9) DMI7 G7

CMA7 DMI7 G7 CMA7 EMI7 A7 DMI7 G7

SOLOS (3 CHORUSES)

C6 SOLO BREAK CMA7 DMI7 G7 CMA7 DMI7 G7 CMA7 DMI7

EMI7 A7
DMI7
BMI7(b5) E7(b9)
AMI7
BMI7(b5)
E7(b9)
AMI7
D7(b5)
DMI7
G7
GMI7
C7
FMA7
FMI7
Bb7
C6/E A7
DMI7 G7
CMA7
DMI7 G7
CMA7
EMI7 A7
DMI7
G7
C6
DMI7 G7
CMA7
DMI7 G7SUS
CMA7
DMI7 G7
CMA7 DMI7
EMI7 A7
DMI7
BMI7(b5) E7(b9)
AMI7
BMI7(b5)
E7(b9)
AMI7
D7
DMI7
G7
GMI7
C7
FMA7
FMI7
Bb7
C6/E A7
DMI7 G7
CMA7
DMI7 G7
CMA7
EMI7 A7
DMI7
G7
FMI7 Bb7 EMI7 A7
DMI7
G7
C6
CMA7(b5)

CD
(17): SPLIT TRACK/MELODY
(18): FULL STEREO TRACK

THE NIGHT HAS A THOUSAND EYES

WORDS BY BUDDY BERNIER
MUSIC BY JERRY BRAININ

𝄢: C VERSION

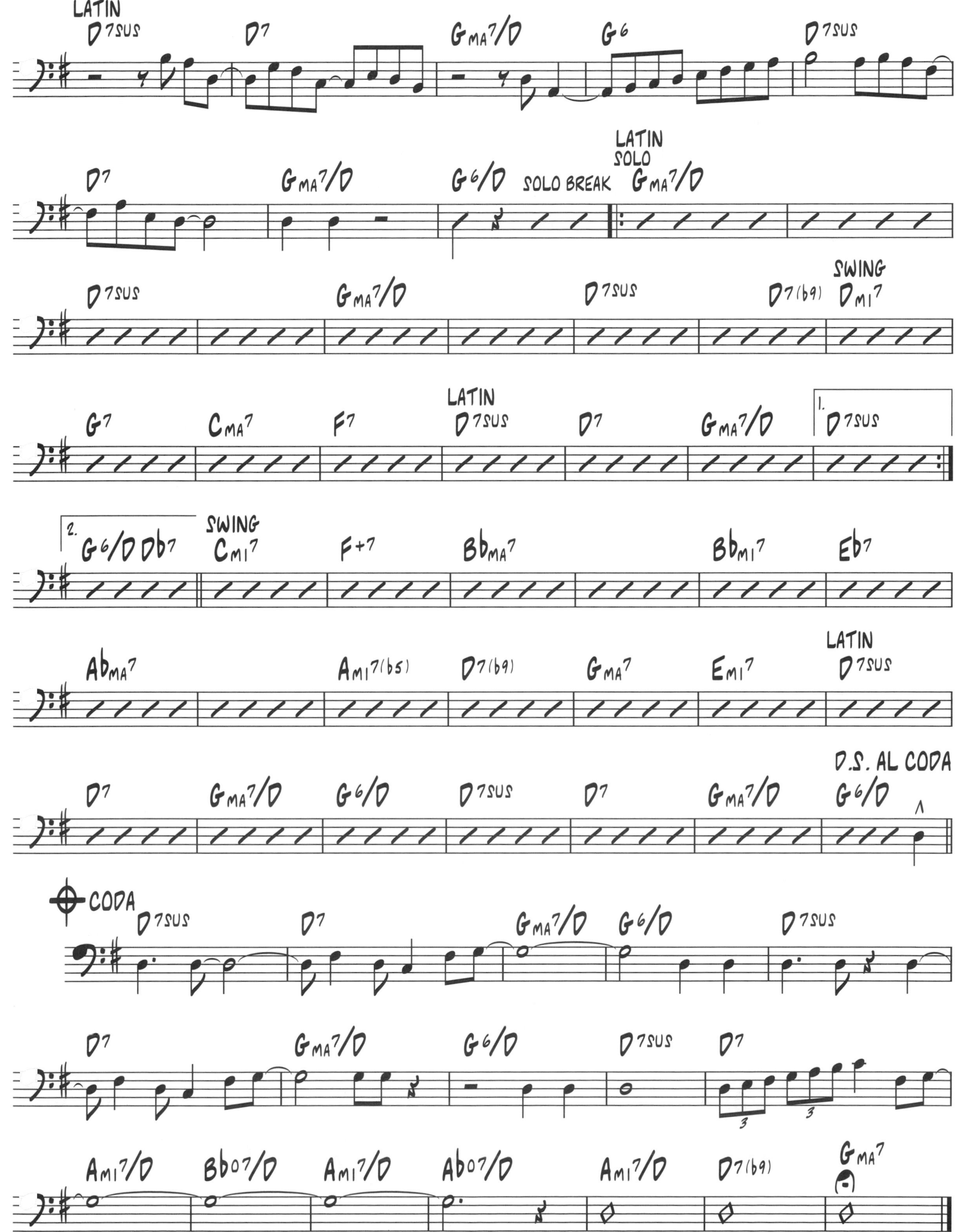
LATIN
D7SUS
D7
GMA7/D
G6
D7SUS
D7
GMA7/D
G6/D
SOLO BREAK
LATIN
SOLO
GMA7/D
D7SUS
GMA7/D
D7SUS
D7(b9)
SWING
DMI7
G7
CMA7
F7
LATIN
D7SUS
D7
GMA7/D
1.
D7SUS
2.
G6/D Db7
SWING
CMI7
F+7
BbMA7
BbMI7
Eb7
AbMA7
AMI7(b5)
D7(b9)
GMA7
EMI7
LATIN
D7SUS
D7
GMA7/D
G6/D
D7SUS
D7
GMA7/D
D.S. AL CODA
G6/D
CODA
D7SUS
D7
GMA7/D
G6/D
D7SUS
D7
GMA7/D
G6/D
D7SUS
D7
AMI7/D
Bbo7/D
AMI7/D
Abo7/D
AMI7/D
D7(b9)
GMA7

CD
19 : SPLIT TRACK/MELODY
20 : FULL STEREO TRACK

SOFTLY AS IN A MORNING SUNRISE

LYRICS BY OSCAR HAMMERSTEIN II
MUSIC BY SIGMUND ROMBERG

C VERSION

MEDIUM SWING

Cmi7 /Bb Dmi7(b5)/Ab G+7 Cmi7 Eb7 Dmi7(b5) G+7

mf

Cmi7 /Bb Dmi7(b5)/Ab G+7 Cmi7 Db7(b5) Dmi7(b5) G+7(#9)

Cmi7 /Bb Dmi7(b5)/Ab G+7 Cmi7 Eb7 Dmi7(b5) G+7

Cmi7 /Bb Dmi7(b5)/Ab G+7 Cmi7 Fmi7 Bb7

Ebma7 E°7

Fmi7 F#°7 G7 Dmi7(b5) Ab7 G7(b9)

Cmi7 /Bb Dmi7(b5)/Ab G+7 Cmi7 Eb7 Dmi7(b5) G+7

SOLOS (3 CHORUSES)
CMI7
DMI7(b5) G+7
CMI7
DMI7(b5) G+7
CMI7
DMI7(b5) G+7
CMI7 Db7(b5)
DMI7(b5) G+7(#9)
CMI7
DMI7(b5) G+7
CMI7
DMI7(b5) G+7
CMI7
DMI7(b5) G+7
CMI7
FMI7 Bb7
EbMA7
Db7(b5)
C7(b9)
FMI7
F#o7
D7(#9)
G+7
CMI7
DMI7(b5) G+7
CMI7
DMI7(b5) G+7
D.C. AL CODA
CMI7
DMI7(b5) G+7
CMI7 Db7(b5)
DMI7(b5) Db7(b5)
CODA
N.C.
CMI(MA7)
DRUMS

Presenting the Hal Leonard JAZZ PLAY-ALONG® SERIES

For use with all B-flat, E-flat, Bass Clef and C instruments, the Jazz Play-Along® Series is the ultimate learning tool for all jazz musicians. With musician-friendly lead sheets, melody cues, and other split-track choices on the included CD, these first-of-a-kind packages help you master improvisation while playing some of the greatest tunes of all time. FOR STUDY, each tune includes a split track with: melody cue with proper style and inflection • professional rhythm tracks • choruses for soloing • removable bass part • removable piano part. FOR PERFORMANCE, each tune also has: an additional full stereo accompaniment track (no melody) • additional choruses for soloing.

1A. MAIDEN VOYAGE/ALL BLUES
00843158 .... $15.99

1. DUKE ELLINGTON
00841644 .... $16.95

2. MILES DAVIS
00841645 .... $16.95

3. THE BLUES
00841646 .... $16.99

4. JAZZ BALLADS
00841691 .... $16.99

5. BEST OF BEBOP
00841689 .... $16.95

6. JAZZ CLASSICS WITH EASY CHANGES
00841690 .... $16.99

7. ESSENTIAL JAZZ STANDARDS
00843000 .... $16.99

8. ANTONIO CARLOS JOBIM AND THE ART OF THE BOSSA NOVA
00843001 .... $16.95

9. DIZZY GILLESPIE
00843002 .... $16.99

10. DISNEY CLASSICS
00843003 .... $16.99

11. RODGERS AND HART FAVORITES
00843004 .... $16.99

12. ESSENTIAL JAZZ CLASSICS
00843005 .... $16.99

13. JOHN COLTRANE
00843006 .... $16.95

14. IRVING BERLIN
00843007 .... $15.99

15. RODGERS & HAMMERSTEIN
00843008 .... $15.99

16. COLE PORTER
00843009 .... $15.95

17. COUNT BASIE
00843010 .... $16.95

18. HAROLD ARLEN
00843011 .... $15.95

19. COOL JAZZ
00843012 .... $15.95

20. CHRISTMAS CAROLS
00843080 .... $14.95

21. RODGERS AND HART CLASSICS
00843014 .... $14.95

22. WAYNE SHORTER
00843015 .... $16.95

23. LATIN JAZZ
00843016 .... $16.95

24. EARLY JAZZ STANDARDS
00843017 .... $14.95

25. CHRISTMAS JAZZ
00843018 .... $16.95

26. CHARLIE PARKER
00843019 .... $16.95

27. GREAT JAZZ STANDARDS
00843020 .... $16.99

28. BIG BAND ERA
00843021 .... $15.99

29. LENNON AND MCCARTNEY
00843022 .... $16.95

30. BLUES' BEST
00843023 .... $15.99

31. JAZZ IN THREE
00843024 .... $15.99

32. BEST OF SWING
00843025 .... $15.99

33. SONNY ROLLINS
00843029 .... $15.95

34. ALL TIME STANDARDS
00843030 .... $15.99

35. BLUESY JAZZ
00843031 .... $16.99

36. HORACE SILVER
00843032 .... $16.99

37. BILL EVANS
00843033 .... $16.95

38. YULETIDE JAZZ
00843034 .... $16.95

39. "ALL THE THINGS YOU ARE" & MORE JEROME KERN SONGS
00843035 .... $15.99

40. BOSSA NOVA
00843036 .... $16.99

41. CLASSIC DUKE ELLINGTON
00843037 .... $16.99

42. GERRY MULLIGAN FAVORITES
00843038 .... $16.99

43. GERRY MULLIGAN CLASSICS
00843039 .... $16.99

44. OLIVER NELSON
00843040 .... $16.95

45. GEORGE GERSHWIN
00103643 .... $24.99

46. BROADWAY JAZZ STANDARDS
00843042 .... $15.99

47. CLASSIC JAZZ BALLADS
00843043 .... $15.99

48. BEBOP CLASSICS
00843044 .... $16.99

49. MILES DAVIS STANDARDS
00843045 .... $16.95

50. GREAT JAZZ CLASSICS
00843046 .... $15.99

51. UP-TEMPO JAZZ
00843047 .... $15.99

52. STEVIE WONDER
00843048 .... $16.99

53. RHYTHM CHANGES
00843049 .... $15.99

54. "MOONLIGHT IN VERMONT" AND OTHER GREAT STANDARDS
00843050 .... $15.99

55. BENNY GOLSON
00843052 .... $15.95

56. "GEORGIA ON MY MIND" & OTHER SONGS BY HOAGY CARMICHAEL
00843056 .... $15.99

57. VINCE GUARALDI
00843057 .... $16.99

58. MORE LENNON AND MCCARTNEY
00843059 .... $16.99

59. SOUL JAZZ
00843060 .... $16.99

60. DEXTER GORDON
00843061 .... $15.95

61. MONGO SANTAMARIA
00843062 .... $15.95

62. JAZZ-ROCK FUSION
00843063 .... $16.99

63. CLASSICAL JAZZ
00843064 .... $14.95

64. TV TUNES
00843065 .... $14.95

65. SMOOTH JAZZ
00843066 .... $16.99

66. A CHARLIE BROWN CHRISTMAS
00843067 .... $16.99

67. CHICK COREA
00843068 .... $15.95

68. CHARLES MINGUS
00843069 .... $16.95

69. CLASSIC JAZZ
00843071 .... $15.99

70. THE DOORS
00843072 .... $14.95

71. COLE PORTER CLASSICS
00843073 .... $14.95

72. CLASSIC JAZZ BALLADS
00843074 .... $15.99

73. JAZZ/BLUES
00843075 $14.95

74. BEST JAZZ CLASSICS
00843076 $15.99

75. PAUL DESMOND
00843077 $16.99

76. BROADWAY JAZZ BALLADS
00843078 $15.99

77. JAZZ ON BROADWAY
00843079 $15.99

78. STEELY DAN
00843070 $15.99

79. MILES DAVIS CLASSICS
00843081 $15.99

80. JIMI HENDRIX
00843083 $16.99

81. FRANK SINATRA – CLASSICS
00843084 $15.99

82. FRANK SINATRA – STANDARDS
00843085 $16.99

83. ANDREW LLOYD WEBBER
00843104 $14.95

84. BOSSA NOVA CLASSICS
00843105 $14.95

85. MOTOWN HITS
00843109 $14.95

86. BENNY GOODMAN
00843110 $15.99

87. DIXIELAND
00843111 $16.99

88. DUKE ELLINGTON FAVORITES
00843112 $14.95

89. IRVING BERLIN FAVORITES
00843113 $14.95

90. THELONIOUS MONK CLASSICS
00841262 $16.99

91. THELONIOUS MONK FAVORITES
00841263 $16.99

92. LEONARD BERNSTEIN
00450134 $15.99

93. DISNEY FAVORITES
00843142 $14.99

94. RAY
00843143 $14.99

95. JAZZ AT THE LOUNGE
00843144 $14.99

96. LATIN JAZZ STANDARDS
00843145 $15.99

97. MAYBE I'M AMAZED*
00843148 $15.99

98. DAVE FRISHBERG
00843149 $15.99

99. SWINGING STANDARDS
00843150 $14.99

100. LOUIS ARMSTRONG
00740423 $16.99

101. BUD POWELL
00843152 $14.99

102. JAZZ POP
00843153 $15.99

103. ON GREEN DOLPHIN STREET & OTHER JAZZ CLASSICS
00843154 $14.99

104. ELTON JOHN
00843155 $14.99

105. SOULFUL JAZZ
00843151 $15.99

106. SLO' JAZZ
00843117 $14.99

107. MOTOWN CLASSICS
00843116 $14.99

108. JAZZ WALTZ
00843159 $15.99

109. OSCAR PETERSON
00843160 $16.99

110. JUST STANDARDS
00843161 $15.99

111. COOL CHRISTMAS
00843162 $15.99

112. PAQUITO D'RIVERA – LATIN JAZZ*
48020662 $16.99

113. PAQUITO D'RIVERA – BRAZILIAN JAZZ*
48020663 $19.99

114. MODERN JAZZ QUARTET FAVORITES
00843163 $15.99

115. THE SOUND OF MUSIC
00843164 $15.99

116. JACO PASTORIUS
00843165 $15.99

117. ANTONIO CARLOS JOBIM – MORE HITS
00843166 $15.99

118. BIG JAZZ STANDARDS COLLECTION
00843167 $27.50

119. JELLY ROLL MORTON
00843168 $15.99

120. J.S. BACH
00843169 $15.99

121. DJANGO REINHARDT
00843170 $15.99

122. PAUL SIMON
00843182 $16.99

123. BACHARACH & DAVID
00843185 $15.99

124. JAZZ-ROCK HORN HITS
00843186 $15.99

126. COUNT BASIE CLASSICS
00843157 $15.99

127. CHUCK MANGIONE
00843188 $15.99

128. VOCAL STANDARDS (LOW VOICE)
00843189 $15.99

129. VOCAL STANDARDS (HIGH VOICE)
00843190 $15.99

130. VOCAL JAZZ (LOW VOICE)
00843191 $15.99

131. VOCAL JAZZ (HIGH VOICE)
00843192 $15.99

132. STAN GETZ ESSENTIALS
00843193 $15.99

133. STAN GETZ FAVORITES
00843194 $15.99

134. NURSERY RHYMES*
00843196 $17.99

135. JEFF BECK
00843197 $15.99

136. NAT ADDERLEY
00843198 $15.99

137. WES MONTGOMERY
00843199 $15.99

138. FREDDIE HUBBARD
00843200 $15.99

139. JULIAN "CANNONBALL" ADDERLEY
00843201 $15.99

140. JOE ZAWINUL
00843202 $15.99

141. BILL EVANS STANDARDS
00843156 $15.99

142. CHARLIE PARKER GEMS
00843222 $15.99

*These CDs do not include split tracks.

143. JUST THE BLUES
00843223 $15.99

144. LEE MORGAN
00843229 $15.99

145. COUNTRY STANDARDS
00843230 $15.99

146. RAMSEY LEWIS
00843231 $15.99

147. SAMBA
00843232 $15.99

150. JAZZ IMPROV BASICS
00843195 $19.99

151. MODERN JAZZ QUARTET CLASSICS
00843209 $15.99

152. J.J. JOHNSON
00843210 $15.99

154. HENRY MANCINI
00843213 $14.99

155. SMOOTH JAZZ CLASSICS
00843215 $15.99

156. THELONIOUS MONK – EARLY GEMS
00843216 $15.99

157. HYMNS
00843217 $15.99

158. JAZZ COVERS ROCK
00843219 $15.99

159. MOZART
00843220 $15.99

160. GEORGE SHEARING
14041531 $16.99

161. DAVE BRUBECK
14041556 $16.99

162. BIG CHRISTMAS COLLECTION
00843221 $24.99

164. HERB ALPERT
14041775 $16.99

165. GEORGE BENSON
00843240 $16.99

167. JOHNNY MANDEL
00103642 $16.99

168. TADD DAMERON
00103663 $15.99

169. BEST JAZZ STANDARDS
00109249 $19.99

170. ULTIMATE JAZZ STANDARDS
00109250 $19.99

172. POP STANDARDS
00111669 $15.99

174. TIN PAN ALLEY
00119125 $15.99

175. TANGO
00119836 $15.99

176. JOHNNY MERCER
00119838 $15.99

Prices, contents, and availability subject to change without notice.

HAL•LEONARD®
CORPORATION
7777 W. BLUEMOUND RD. P.O. BOX 13819
MILWAUKEE, WISCONSIN 53213

For complete songlists and more, visit Hal Leonard online at
www.halleonard.com

1013

Jazz Instruction & Improvisation

BOOKS FOR ALL INSTRUMENTS FROM HAL LEONARD

AN APPROACH TO JAZZ IMPROVISATION

by Dave Pozzi
Musicians Institute Press

Explore the styles of Charlie Parker, Sonny Rollins, Bud Powell and others with this comprehensive guide to jazz improvisation. Covers: scale choices • chord analysis • phrasing • melodies • harmonic progressions • more.

00695135 Book/CD Pack..$17.95

THE ART OF MODULATING

FOR PIANISTS AND JAZZ MUSICIANS

by Carlos Salzedo & Lucile Lawrence
Schirmer

The Art of Modulating is a treatise originally intended for the harp, but this edition has been edited for use by intermediate keyboardists and other musicians who have an understanding of basic music theory. In its pages you will find: table of intervals; modulation rules; modulation formulas; examples of modulation; extensions and cadences; ten fragments of dances; five characteristic pieces; and more.

50490581 ....$19.99

BUILDING A JAZZ VOCABULARY

By Mike Steinel

A valuable resource for learning the basics of jazz from Mike Steinel of the University of North Texas. It covers: the basics of jazz • how to build effective solos • a comprehensive practice routine • and a jazz vocabulary of the masters.

00849911 ....$19.95

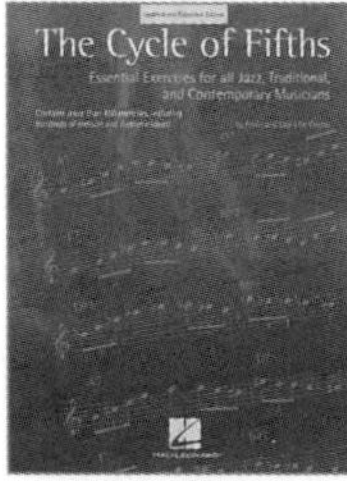

THE CYCLE OF FIFTHS

by Emile and Laura De Cosmo

This essential instruction book provides more than 450 exercises, including hundreds of melodic and rhythmic ideas. The book is designed to help improvisors master the cycle of fifths, one of the primary progressions in music. Guaranteed to refine technique, enhance improvisational fluency, and improve sight-reading!

00311114 ....$16.99

THE DIATONIC CYCLE

by Emile and Laura De Cosmo

Renowned jazz educators Emile and Laura De Cosmo provide more than 300 exercises to help improvisors tackle one of music's most common progressions: the diatonic cycle. This book is guaranteed to refine technique, enhance improvisational fluency, and improve sight-reading!

00311115 ....$16.95

EAR TRAINING

by Keith Wyatt, Carl Schroeder and Joe Elliott
Musicians Institute Press

Covers: basic pitch matching • singing major and minor scales • identifying intervals • transcribing melodies and rhythm • identifying chords and progressions • seventh chords and the blues • modal interchange, chromaticism, modulation • and more.

00695198 Book/2-CD Pack $24.95

EXERCISES AND ETUDES FOR THE JAZZ INSTRUMENTALIST

by J.J. Johnson

Designed as study material and playable by any instrument, these pieces run the gamut of the jazz experience, featuring common and uncommon time signatures and keys, and styles from ballads to funk. They are progressively graded so that both beginners and professionals will be challenged by the demands of this wonderful music.

00842018 Bass Clef Edition $16.95
00842042 Treble Clef Edition $16.95

JAZZOLOGY

THE ENCYCLOPEDIA OF JAZZ THEORY FOR ALL MUSICIANS

by Robert Rawlins and Nor Eddine Bahha

This comprehensive resource covers a variety of jazz topics, for beginners and pros of any instrument. The book serves as an encyclopedia for reference, a thorough methodology for the student, and a workbook for the classroom.

00311167 ....$19.99

JAZZ THEORY RESOURCES

by Bert Ligon
Houston Publishing, Inc.

This is a jazz theory text in two volumes. **Volume 1 includes**: review of basic theory • rhythm in jazz performance • triadic generalization • diatonic harmonic progressions and analysis • substitutions and turnarounds • and more. **Volume 2 includes**: modes and modal frameworks • quartal harmony • extended tertian structures and triadic superimposition • pentatonic applications • coloring "outside" the lines and beyond • and more.

00030458 Volume 1 ....$39.95
00030459 Volume 2 ....$29.95

JOY OF IMPROV

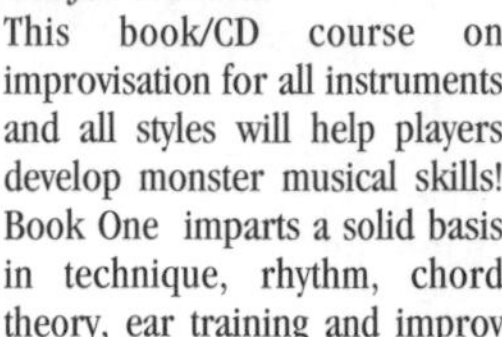

by Dave Frank and John Amaral

This book/CD course on improvisation for all instruments and all styles will help players develop monster musical skills! Book One imparts a solid basis in technique, rhythm, chord theory, ear training and improv concepts. **Book Two** explores more advanced chord voicings, chord arranging techniques and more challenging blues and melodic lines. The CD can be used as a listening and play-along tool.

00220005 Book 1 – Book/CD Pack.......................$27.99
00220006 Book 2 – Book/CD Pack.......................$26.99

THE PATH TO JAZZ IMPROVISATION

by Emile and Laura De Cosmo

This fascinating jazz instruction book offers an innovative, scholarly approach to the art of improvisation. It includes in-depth analysis and lessons about: cycle of fifths • diatonic cycle • overtone series • pentatonic scale • harmonic and melodic minor scale • polytonal order of keys • blues and bebop scales • modes • and more.

00310904 ....$14.99

THE SOURCE

THE DICTIONARY OF CONTEMPORARY AND TRADITIONAL SCALES

by Steve Barta

This book serves as an informative guide for people who are looking for good, solid information regarding scales, chords, and how they work together. It provides right and left hand fingerings for scales, chords, and complete inversions. Includes over 20 different scales, each written in all 12 keys.

00240885 ....$18.99

21 BEBOP EXERCISES

by Steve Rawlins

This book/CD pack is both a warm-up collection and a manual for bebop phrasing. Its tasty and sophisticated exercises will help you develop your proficiency with jazz interpretation. It concentrates on practice in all twelve keys – moving higher by half-step – to help develop dexterity and range. The companion CD includes all of the exercises in 12 keys.

00315341 Book/CD Pack..$17.95

Visit Hal Leonard online at
www.halleonard.com

Prices, contents & availability subject to change without notice.

0113